THE BEST
Front Range
Wildflower
HIKES

MARLENE M. BORNEMAN

The Colorado Mountain Club Press
Golden, Colorado

The Best Front Range Wildflower Hikes
© 2016 by The Colorado Mountain Club

PUBLISHED BY
The Colorado Mountain Club Press
710 Tenth Street, Suite 200, Golden, Colorado 80401
303-996-2743   e-mail: cmcpress@cmc.org

Founded in 1912, The Colorado Mountain Club is the largest outdoor recreation, education, and conservation organization in the Rocky Mountains. Look for our books at your local bookstore or outdoor retailer or online at www.cmc.org/store.

Marlene M. Borneman: author, photographer
Daniel Carver: maps
Jodi Jennings: copy editor
Erika K. Arroyo: design, composition, and production
Sarah Gorecki: publisher

CONTACTING THE PUBLISHER
We would appreciate it if readers would alert us to any errors or outdated information by contacting us at the address above.

DISTRIBUTED TO THE BOOK TRADE BY
The Mountaineers Books, 1001 SW Klickitat Way, Suite 201, Seattle, WA 98134, 800-553-4453, www.mountaineersbooks.org

Topographic maps were created using CalTopo software (caltopo.com).

COVER PHOTO: Wildflower garden at Butler Gulch. Photo by Marlene M. Borneman

We gratefully acknowledge the financial support of the people of Colorado through the Scientific and Cultural Facilities District of greater Denver for our publishing activities.

WARNING: Although there has been an effort to make the trail descriptions in this book as accurate as possible, some discrepancies may exist between the text and the trails in the field. Hiking in mountainous and desert areas is a high-risk activity. This guidebook is not a substitute for your experience and common sense. The users of this guidebook assume full responsibility for their own safety. Weather, terrain conditions, and individual abilities must be considered before undertaking any of the hikes in this guide.

First Edition

ISBN 978-1-937052-31-7
Ebook 978-1-937052-32-4

Printed in Korea

DEDICATION

Where

    flowers

bloom,

    so does

hope.

—Lady Bird Johnson

For my granddaughter, Corina.
Wishing her a lifetime full of wildflowers.

The pika enjoys his favorite food, alpine avens, which turn red in autumn.

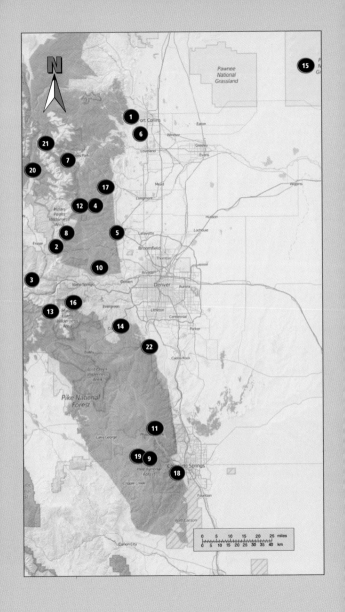

CONTENTS

THE HIKES

An alpine thistle with a rather alien appearance.

ACKNOWLEDGMENTS

First and always, thanks to Walt, my husband, for his staying power and companionship on many of these hikes.

At the top of my acknowledgments is the Colorado Mountain Club, where my interest in Colorado trails bloomed. The CMC provided me with many opportunities, learning experiences, and connections—opening doors to trails and companions.

I am privileged to be a pack guide author contributing to the CMC's mission of education and preservation. I'm grateful for the leadership of Sarah Gorecki, Director of Publishing. Sarah's expert advice and patience guided me through to completion of this book.

The Estes Park Flower Group, an informal but driven group of folks, inspired me to keep learning the technical side of the fascinating world of native wildflowers. I owe a special debt to Marcia Tavel and Dott Dewitz, who assisted me with plant identification and accompanied me in the field over the years. Special thanks to Jennifer Ackerfield, author of *Flora of Colorado*, for a quick response in clarifying a species; to Katy Sykes, Rocky Mountain National Park, Manager, Information Office; and Megan Bowes, Restoration Plant Ecologist, for reviewing parts of this pack guide.

I am also thankful for the Colorado Native Plant Society, a tremendous resource on Colorado's native flora and habitats. CoNPS provides workshops, field trips, and environmental news, advancing their mission of education, stewardship, and advocacy.

I always appreciate the enlightening conversations with Al Schneider. His website is chock full of valuable information to help identify plants and find detailed facts about each one.

Finally, many thanks to the US Forest Service, National Park Service, and state and county parks employees and volunteers who work to protect and maintain these flora-filled trails.

FOREWORD

Hiking to identify flowers, find an uncommon plant, or add to a life list is a gratifying adventure for both body and mind. Staying safe and protecting Colorado's flora are essential elements of the enjoyment.

RATINGS

Hike ratings consider mileage as well as elevation gain and type of terrain. Mileages alone can be misleading. For example, a 2-mile hike on uneven rocky terrain with 1,000 feet of elevation gain will be more difficult than a 4-mile hike on level terrain with 300 feet of elevation gain.

ROUND-TRIP TIME

Typical round-trip time is based on hiking two miles per hour; however, time has been added to allow for frequent stops to identify and photograph plants. Round-trip times depend on an individual's physical ability and number of rest stops taken. Adjust accordingly.

SAFETY

It is each individual's responsibility to know the risks and be prepared. A good practice is to leave a detailed itinerary of the day's plan with a responsible person, including your intended trailhead, hiking trail, and expected time of return. See the Ten Essentials Systems for a list of items to carry while hiking.

WEATHER

Ever-changing is the weather motto in Colorado. Check the local forecast, start early to avoid afternoon thunderstorms, and be prepared with multiple layers and rain gear.

The stunning rare wood lily is enjoyed by a swallowtail butterfly.

PROTECT THE FLORA

Never pick wildflowers! Do not attempt to transplant wild plants, especially orchids and lilies. These plants may be endangered and require specialized habitats that Mother Nature provides. It is illegal to collect plants in the national parks and national forests. An option is to purchase native plants from reputable plant nurseries. Al Schneider, creator of www.swcoloradowildflowers.com, says it best: "Admire them in the wild and let them live."

LEAVE NO TRACE

We owe it to present and future generations to care for the wild places. If you pack it in, pack it out—leave only footprints:

- Plan ahead and prepare for the cleanest possible adventure.
- Stay on the trail and don't shortcut the switchbacks. Camp on durable surfaces, such as rock or sand. If more than one person goes off trail, spread out so you don't start destructive new "social" trails.
- Dispose of all waste properly, including that deposited by your dog. "Pack it in, pack it out."

- Leave what you find and don't pick it up—look at it, take a photo, leave it for the next person.
- Minimize campfire impacts—keep any fires small and keep the fuel within the fire circle. Unless it is a permanent fire pit, destroy all traces of your fire before leaving your campsite. Forest fires have started from small campfires or their smoldering embers; be extremely cautious in this regard. The best practice is to completely soak down your fire site.
- Respect wildlife. Don't feed animals anything and don't intrude on their feeding and breeding areas.
- Be considerate of animals and other humans on the trail—don't play your radio or make other unnecessary noise. Part of the allure of the outdoors is the healing sound of the wind through the trees and the murmur of a stream.

Caveat—on maps and map scales

In producing this pack guide, we have endeavored to provide the most accurate information possible. This striving for accuracy includes the map segments that follow each trail description. Many of the trails indicated by the red lines, however, include contours, ups and downs, and switchbacks that cannot be depicted on a small map. Thus, with some maps, you may find what looks like a variance between the stated length of the trail and the length of the trail when compared to the scale indicator.

For every trail described in this guide, we list relevant, larger-scale maps of the area you will be hiking in—such as Trails Illustrated and USGS maps. It is always a good practice to secure these larger maps, study them, and understand where the smaller map from the guide fits within the larger map. The best practice is to carry both maps on your hike.

Resources

Colorado Mountain Club: www.cmc.org
Colorado Native Plant Society: www.conps.org
Colorado State University Extension: www.conativeplantmaster.org
Rocky Mountain Conservancy: https://rmconservancy.org
www.swcoloradowildflowers.com
Ackerfield, Jennifer, *Flora of Colorado*, Fort Worth, TX: BRIT Press, 2015

Introduction

Every year, dazzling wildflowers string a necklace of color across the plains and the mountains of Colorado's Front Range. This pack guide provides descriptions of twenty-two wildflower-filled hikes in the Front Range, steering you in the right direction to enjoy old favorites and discover new, less commonly seen species.

Plants grow within layers of altitude, referred to as life zones. Colorado has five life zones where approximately 700 species of plants flourish on the Front Range. Since life zones do not have clear-cut boundaries, flora often overlap these life zones.

Remember that seasonal appearances sometimes vary by weeks from year to year. Nature strictly controls blooming times at all elevations with temperature and moisture. These variables influence a bountiful season or a stingy one. In this pack guide, "peak bloom" refers to the most likely time to view a wide range of flowers with the greatest numbers in bloom. Keep in mind that there will always be early and late blooming flowers before and after peak bloom. These ever-changing wildflower blooms make every outing fresh and stimulating.

Common names are used in this text; however, be mindful that one flower can have several common names. Common names originate from a local region or generation era. To assure clear communication, check the Appendix for the scientific names. Learning the scientific

Blue-eyed grass is a lovely deep blue, often found hidden among taller grasses.

A bouquet of fireweed brightens late summer.

family names and family characteristics is very helpful in identification of and communication about plants.

The goal of *The Best Front Range Wildflower Hikes* is to guide you to a variety of habitats producing a diversity of flowers. "Best," of course, is a subjective term. Every effort has been made to include trails across multiple life zones, providing many opportunities to view and identify a wide range of wildflowers. Easy access to the trailheads was considered to allow you to spend more time with the flowers rather than trying to reach them. Each hike offers an unexpected "wow" factor, making for a memorable moment. Much effort has been made to correctly identify wildflower species. Comments are welcome on any misidentified species or other errors in this guide. Whatever trail you decide to explore, simply delight in this world filled with wildflowers!

COLORADO LIFE ZONES

Plains: 3,500–6,500 feet
Foothills: 6,500–8,000 feet
Montane: 8,000–10,000 feet
Subalpine: 10,000–11,500 feet
Alpine: above 11,500 feet

The Ten Essentials Systems

The Colorado Mountain Club (CMC), through CMC Press, is the publisher of this pack guide. For over 100 years, CMC has fostered safety awareness and safe practices in the wilderness, and has distilled the essential safety items down to a list known as "The Ten Essentials." We present it here in a "systems" approach. Carrying the items from this list that are appropriate for the location, mileage, and elevation of your hike will help you be fully prepared for every trip and able to survive the unexpected emergency. We encourage all hikers to study, adopt, and teach The Ten Essentials Systems as part of their own outdoors regimen.

1. **Hydration.** Carry at least 2 liters or quarts of water on any hike. Keep an extra water container in your vehicle and hydrate both before and after your hike. Don't wait until you are thirsty—stay hydrated.

2. **Nutrition.** Eat a good breakfast before your hike; pack a full and healthy lunch, including fruits, vegetables, and carbohydrates. Carry healthy snacks such as trail mix and nutrition bars.

3. **Sun protection.** Start with sunscreen with an SFP rating of at least 45 and reapply it as you hike. Wear sunglasses and a wide-brimmed hat, and use lip balm. These protections are important anywhere in Colorado, especially at high elevations.

4. **Insulation.** Be aware that weather in Colorado can go through extreme changes in a very short time. Dress with wool or synthetic inner and outer layers. Cotton retains moisture and does not insulate well; it should not be part of your hiking gear. Carry a warm hat, gloves, and extra socks. Always include a

rain/wind parka and rain pants—on you or in your pack. Extra clothing weighs little and is a great safety component.

5. **Navigation.** You should attain at least minimal proficiency with a map and compass. A GPS unit can add to your ability, but it's not a substitute for the two basics. Before a hike, study your route, and the surrounding country, on a good map of the area. Refer to the map as needed on the trail.

6. **Illumination.** Include a headlamp or flashlight in your gear, preferably both. With a headlamp, your hands are kept free. Avoid hiking in the dark if at all possible.

7. **First Aid.** Buy or assemble an adequate first-aid kit. Some things to include:

   - Ace bandages; a bandana, which can double as a sling.
   - Duct tape—good for a bandage, blister protection, or rips in your clothes.
   - A small bottle of alcohol or hydrogen peroxide for cleaning a wound.
   - Latex gloves.
   - Specific medications for you and your companions.
   - Toilet paper and sealable plastic bags for carrying it out.

Note: This is not a comprehensive list—tailor it and add items for your own perceived needs and intended activities.

8. **Fire.** The best practice is to avoid open fires except in emergency situations. For when you may need to build a fire, carry waterproof matches in a watertight container, a lighter, or a commercial fire starter such as a fire ribbon. Keep these items dry and ensure that all of them will work in cold or wet weather. If needed, tree sap or dry pine needles can help start a fire.

Black-tipped ragwort and a moth of the *Pterophoidae* family. Wildflowers not only provide stunning scenery but also provide food, shelter, and nesting for many animals and insects.

9. **Repair kit and emergency tools.** A pocketknife or multitool and duct tape or electrician's tape are good for various repairs. For emergencies, carry a whistle and signal mirror.

10. **Emergency shelter.** Carry a space blanket and nylon cord or a bivouac sack. Large plastic leaf bags are handy for temporary rain gear, pack covers, or survival shelters. On your way out, use this for trash left by careless hikers.

1. Arthur's Rock Trail

LORY STATE PARK

MAPS	USGS, Horsetooth Reservoir, 7.5 minute; Recreational Map for Colorado's Horsetooth Mountain Park and Lory State Park, A Mountain Jay Adventure Guide
ELEVATION GAIN	950 feet
RATING	Moderate
ROUND-TRIP DISTANCE	3.6 miles
ROUND-TRIP TIME	4 hours
NEAREST LANDMARK	Horsetooth Reservoir
PEAK BLOOM	Mid-June
LIFE ZONE	Foothills

COMMENT: Arthur's Rock is a prime foothills hike where you can enjoy more than six dozen species of wildflowers. Located within Lory State Park, the hike offers captivating meadows, pine forests, rock formations, and splendid views that ensure a pleasurable outing. The Visitor Center provides maps and checklists of plants and butterflies. The trailhead has ample parking, restrooms, and picnic tables. Dogs are allowed on leash. Be aware: rattlesnakes inhabit this area.

GETTING THERE: This is the most direct and scenic route. From Interstate 25 take Exit 265 for Harmony Road West. Follow Harmony Road west through Fort Collins. At the intersection of Taft Hill Road, Harmony Road becomes County Road 38E. Continue on CR 38E as it winds around and up. At approximately 8.5 miles, at the next intersection, turn right on CR 23S. Drive 1.5 miles to a stop sign. Turn left on Centennial/23N and drive 4.5 miles. Turn left on 25G

Flower-filled meadows with arresting Spiderwort and views of Horsetooth Reservoir.

(Lodgepole Drive). Drive 1.5 miles, turning left at Charles A. Lory State Park. The Visitor Center is ahead on the right. Be prepared to pay a fee. The trailhead is approximately 2 miles past the Visitor Center on a dirt road.

THE ROUTE: The hike begins in a gulch with a seasonal stream providing a gateway to wild roses, Drummond's milkvetch, yellow hawkweed, early blue daisies, nodding onion, cow parsnip, and the lemon-colored leafy cinquefoil. Ninebark shrubs are abundant. The soft pink Fremont geranium and the rougher scorpion weed bloom alongside bluemist penstemon. The striking bluemist penstemon's bright green leaves and flowers, which grow on all sides of the stem, make it distinguishable from other penstemons. Yellow sulphurflowers and stonecrop grow side by side on the hillsides.

Spiderwort plant.

Switchbacks lead to a ponderosa pine forest, home to mouse-ear chickweed, lambstounge, early larkspur, one-sided penstemon, and whiskbroom parsley. Natural rock gardens create habitat for the prickly pear cactus.

Stay left at the Overlook Trail junction, where it is 1.4 miles to Arthur's Rock. Early spring season brings pasqueflowers, snowball saxifrage, clematis, and a gathering of sugarbowls along here. In July, horsemint (beebalm) and the delicate willowherb flourish. Mountain harebells and pussytoes border the trail as you continue up. Rock crannies provide footholds for the common alumroot and spotted saxifrage.

The trail soon meanders through a sizeable meadow where lupine dominates in mid-summer. American vetch and houndstongue, a noxious weed, also appear. A footbridge brings you to the orange and yellow hues of the wallflower. Golden banner, more Fremont geraniums, and wild roses appear. The spiderwort's brilliant royal purple face stands out in these large meadows.

Stay right at the Mill Creek link. Along this section, meadow death camas, scarlet guara, Fendler's senecio, columbines, and tall pussytoes come together. Before long, a serene forest emerges with a seasonal stream that holds Canadian violets along its banks.

Continue up switchbacks with a fusion of deep blues and purples, the result of a mixture of penstemon and Lambert's locoweed. Ahead, meadows continue to overflow with a palette of colors created by spiderwort, miner's candles, bush sunflowers, salsify, blanketflower, larkspur, and yucca. The trail comes to a rocky section where a trail sign marks 0.6 mile to Arthur's Rock. Take time to walk out to the scenic overlook here, where views of Horsetooth Reservoir and beyond are a grand backdrop to the colorful scene.

Colorful Lambert's loco and penstemon along the trail.

Butterfly on a composite flower.

The trail then zigzags through forest, open meadows, and rock outcroppings as the variety of flowers continues. An occasional clump of stemless evening primrose may appear. You may be distracted from the steepness of the trail by the spectrum of flowers, beautiful views, and sightings of butterflies!

Stay right at the junction for the Timber Campsites. The trail ends here at the base of Arthur's Rock. To continue to the summit, scramble up the short, steep, boulder-filled gully and enjoy the panoramic view from Arthur's Rock summit (6,780 feet). Retrace your steps to return to the trailhead.

Penstemons on the summit.

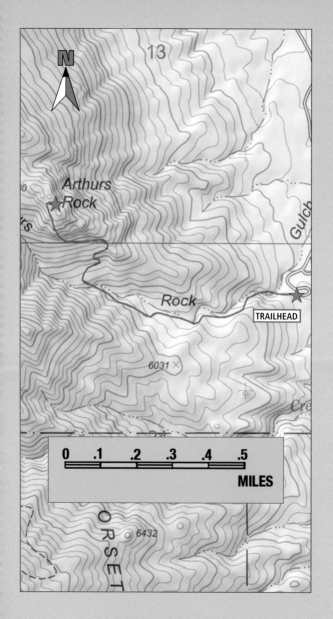

13

Arthurs
Rock

Gulch

Rock

TRAILHEAD

6031 ×

0   .1   .2   .3   .4   .5

MILES

ORSET

6432

2. Bob and Betty Lakes Trail

INDIAN PEAKS WILDERNESS

MAPS	Trails Illustrated, Winter Park/ Central City/Rollins Pass, Number 103; USGS, East Portal, 7.5 minute
ELEVATION GAIN	450 feet out; 500 feet return
RATING	Moderate–moderately strenuous
ROUND-TRIP DISTANCE	4 miles
ROUND-TRIP TIME	3–4 hours
NEAREST LANDMARK	Winter Park Ski Area
PEAK BLOOM	Mid-July–August
LIFE ZONE	Alpine

COMMENT: Bob, Betty, and King Lakes are pristine alpine lakes nestled in a stunning alpine cirque shrouded by a multitude of wildflowers. Although the dirt road leading to the trailhead is rugged and slow going, it is worth the effort. The route described is from the west at Corona/Rollins Pass; this is a longer drive but a shorter hike than from the east.

Corona/Rollins Pass offers a bit of Colorado railroad history. The Winter Park Visitor Center provides a brochure describing historical markers along the road. Wildflowers and wildlife can be spotted on the drive.

The hike is rated moderate to moderately strenuous due to the elevation losses and gains in each direction at altitudes over 11,000 feet. Keep a close watch for afternoon thunderstorms. Dogs are allowed on leash. There are no restrooms at the trailhead.

GETTING THERE: Take Interstate 70 west to the exit for US 40. Drive over Berthoud Pass and past the Winter Park Ski Area. Take a right on Forest Service Road 149, marked Rollins Pass.

Western yellow paintbrush on the High Lonesome Trail.

This is a rutted dirt road; however, most two-wheel-drive passenger cars can drive to the top. It is approximately 14 miles from US 40 to the trailhead. The parking at Corona/Rollins Pass is at 11,660 feet.

THE ROUTE: Follow the High Lonesome Trail northwest past the sign for Indian Peaks Wilderness. The tundra spreads out before you. A treasure trove of flora awaits: moss campion, forget-me-not, alpine sandwort, rose (Northern) gentian, alpine avens, alpine sage, Parry's clover, mouse-ear chickweed, western yellow paintbrush, and alpine sunflowers. Bistort provides a snowy white carpet on the tundra.

At 0.3 mile the junction for King Lake appears on the right. Hike down, losing 200 feet of elevation to King Lake. Even in July there may be snow on the trail. If so, be careful working your way down. The snowfields surrounding this expansive cirque provide for rich and diverse flower communities. Pinnateleaf daisy, stonecrop, alpine sorrel, alpine buttercups,

Bob Lake: a striking scene.

dwarf chiming bells, king's crown, sky pilot, blackhead daisy, and mountain dryad are a few of the gems found on the trail. These high slopes also nurture the tiny alp lily. Mounds of gold sunspots stand out. King Lake's shores are loaded with the colorful hues of paintbrush and rose crown. In August, arctic gentian grows abundantly. Look on the south shore for the delicate alpine starwort. Rocky slopes provide habitat for goldbloom saxifrage, spotted saxifrage, and the alpine big-rooted spring beauty. This astounding alpine plant life scene gets better with each step.

Leaving King Lake, the trail continues down, reaching krummholz and willows. Alpine speedwell, scarlet paintbrush, rosy paintbrush, triangularleaf senecio, subalpine daisies, Gray angelica, mountain death camas, sickletop lousewort, blue violets, mountain candytuft, columbines, and shades of the Whipple's penstemon generate a maze of colors.

Soon you come to the South Fork of Middle Boulder Creek. This stream can be tricky to negotiate; wander downstream to find a safe crossing. Marsh marigolds, brook saxifrage,

View of King Lake from high along the trail.

Rosy paintbrush surrounds King Lake.

caltha-flowered butter-cups, globeflowers, and Parry's primroses are content nearby.

After crossing the stream, find a faint trail angling right through krummholz. The climb starts here, and you will gain 450 feet within approximately 1.0 mile to Bob Lake. On the way, bracted lousewort emerges while Jacob's ladder enjoys the shade of stunted trees.

Alpine meadows open with Betty Lake in sight. Walk around the west shore of Betty Lake to spot the deep purple star gentian and pink mountain laurel. Follow a faint trail on the west side where elephantella stands. You will hear a stream before you see it flowing down to Betty Lake; cross this small stream, following the faint trail while picking your way up through boulders to Bob Lake, a mind-boggling setting.

Cooled by breezes off the snowfields, you can explore the shore of Bob Lake for purple fringe, alpine avens, columbines, and much more. Spot the suitably named snowlover. Parry's primroses grow in masses along the outlet stream rushing to Betty Lake below.

Retrace your steps back to the creek crossing. On the return you may find a sign for King Lake; this is a good crossing spot. Gain 500 feet hiking back to the saddle/junction above King Lake and turn left back to the parking lot.

3. Butler Gulch

ARAPAHO NATIONAL FOREST

MAPS	Trails Illustrated, Winter Park/Central City/Rollins Pass, Number 103; USGS, Berthoud Pass, 7.5 minute
ELEVATION GAIN	1,500 feet
RATING	Moderate
ROUND-TRIP DISTANCE	5.2 miles
ROUND-TRIP TIME	3–5 hours
NEAREST LANDMARK	Henderson Mine
PEAK BLOOM	Mid-July–August
LIFE ZONE	Montane/subalpine/alpine

COMMENT: Butler Gulch is an essential hike for the wildflower devotee, with more than 100 species thriving among the streams, seeps, and high meadows. The trail follows an old mining road with steep sections and several stream crossings. Beware that this trail is often extremely muddy. Your efforts will be rewarded with views of flower-filled meadows stretching out before you framed by the Continental Divide. The trail also offers a snapshot of Colorado's mining history at the ruins of Jean Mine, where old mining machinery, remnants of the abandoned mine, are now part of this landscape.

Start early, as parking near the gate is limited. The hike tops out in the alpine zone, so an early start will also help you avoid afternoon thunderstorms. Dogs are allowed on leash. There are no restrooms.

GETTING THERE: From Interstate 70 west take Exit 232 (US 40 west). Turn right on US 40 and drive through the town of Empire. Drive approximately 7 miles to the Henderson

Colorful high meadows.

Mine/Jones Pass turnoff, turning left at Big Bend Picnic Area, County Road 202 (Henderson Mine/Jones Pass Road). Drive approximately 1.9 miles. Just before the entrance to the Henderson Mine, bear right on a dirt road and drive 0.6 mile to the trailhead on the left. The trail begins at the gate.

THE ROUTE: This wildflower journey features a kaleidoscope of colors from start to finish. As you set out from your car, stands of aspen sunflowers, paintbrushes, and mountain harebells welcome you. In late summer fireweed joins in. Go past the gate and follow the road crossing over the West Fork

Colorful mix in Butler Gulch.

of Clear Creek. Begin to look for the tiny lavender colored rose (northern) gentian. Continue along the shaded road, taking in creamy Whipple's penstemons, subalpine daisies, speedwell, heartleaf arnica, Jacob's ladder, caltha-flowered buttercup, and sickletop lousewort. Nearby, macoun buttercups make an appearance. Spot the easily missed wood nymph in this shaded forest.

Explore the small meadows on the left following the creek. Heartleaf bittercress, marsh marigold, globeflower, bistort, elephantella, cow parsnip, larkspur, and Parry's primrose appear in inexhaustible masses. Here, too, you will find mountain death camas, rosy paintbrush, and bracted lousewort.

Masses of larkspur and chiming bells.

Soon stream crossings and seeps become frequent, but timbers have been placed to help you negotiate them. The inconspicuous Bishop's cap can be seen in these wet areas. This plant, of the *Saxifragaceae* family, sports unusual tiny green flowers. The ongoing parade of flowers ahead includes blueleaf cinquefoil, yellow western paintbrush, triangularleaf senecio, and brook saxifrage.

Cross a sizeable stream on a bridge of fallen trees. Stands of bracted lousewort, paintbrush, monkshood, Gray angelica, and larkspur come into view. Multitudes of lovely Colorado columbines alongside waist-high chiming bells make a striking scene. You will pass an occasional bunch of blackhead daisies along the way.

At about one mile, as the trail climbs, watch for a tall, topless, dead tree on the right. Near here on the left lives

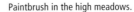
Paintbrush in the high meadows.

an uncommon member of the *Saxifragaceae* family: side-flowered white mitrewort. This plant is difficult to distinguish unless it is in flower. A hand lens is useful for observing the sophistication of the narrow petals and cup-shaped sepals situated on one side of its straight, fragile stem.

More meadows with columbine, monkshood, larkspur, brookcress, and triangularleaf senecio overpower the scene. At approximately 1.5 miles from the trailhead, on the right, plummeting waters cascade down the slopes, nurturing Parry's primroses and many more varieties of flowers.

The trail switchbacks among quantities of heartleaf bittercress and brook saxifrage before it opens out to a spacious view. Larkspur, chiming bells, king's crown, rose crown, alpine sage, alpine avens, and every shade of paintbrush create colorful rainbows in these high meadows. The Parry's gentian waits until late summer to present itself, blooming along strewn boulders.

Continue through these vibrant meadows until you reach Butler Gulch Creek. Look here for valerian, subalpine buttercups, pygmy bitterroot, snowball saxifrage, and mountain laurel. Cross the creek and hike up to the old mine site.

Cushion plants, moss campion, and alpine sandwort mingle with pinnateleaf daisies, along with alpine sunflowers, alpine goldenrod, alpine willow, and a variety of flowers that put their roots down in these high meadows. Retrace your steps to return to the trailhead.

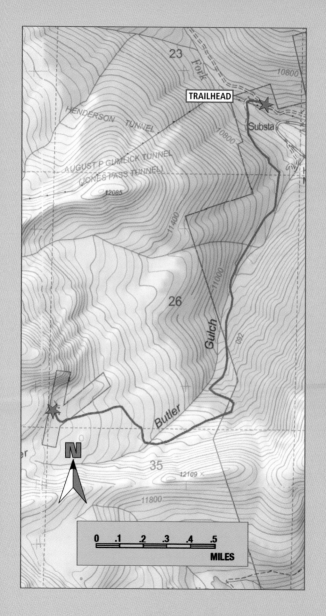

4. Ceran St. Vrain

ROOSEVELT NATIONAL FOREST

MAPS	Trails Illustrated, Boulder/Golden, Number 100 and Indian Peaks/ Gold Hill, Number 102; USGS, Raymond, 7.5 minute
ELEVATION GAIN	250 feet on return
RATING	Easy
ROUND-TRIP DISTANCE	3.6 miles
ROUND-TRIP TIME	3–4 hours
NEAREST LANDMARK	Jamestown
PEAK BLOOM	Early June–mid-July
LIFE ZONE	Foothills/montane

COMMENT: This trail is named for Ceran St. Vrain, a fur trader who explored and established trading posts in this area in the early 1800s. There is a sign at the trailhead that provides interesting facts about this early explorer. South St. Vrain Creek shadows this trek, which supports numerous species, in particular the esteemed fairy slipper orchid. Delight in peaceful hiking in the midst of quaking aspens, lodgepole pines, and Douglas firs, while tranquil sounds of whooshing water accompany you.

Parking fills early on weekends due to the popularity of family camping here. There are no restrooms. Dogs are allowed on a leash.

GETTING THERE: From Boulder, drive north on US 36 for approximately 5 miles and turn left at Lefthand Canyon Road. Drive 8 miles to the small village of Jamestown. Note that at 4.5 miles the road becomes dirt. Drive 5 miles more to the trailhead sign on the right. It is 0.25 mile to parking.

The esteemed fairy slipper orchid.

From Nederland, at the intersection of Colorado 119 and CO 72, drive on CO 72 west for 16 miles to Overland Road. Turn right and drive Overland Road for 1.7 miles. Turn left at the trailhead sign. It is 0.25 mile to parking.

THE ROUTE: Once you locate a parking space, you will immediately begin to spot red anemones, golden smoke, golden draba, and monument plant (green gentian) along the path. Cross a rustic bridge for the real show. Stonecrop, mouse-ear chickweed, star Solomon's seal, false Solomon's seal, clematis, and oodles of heartleaf arnicas fill the area. At the beginning of this hike you will also find the beautiful Fendler's waterleaf plant with whitish to pale lavender flowers. A distinctive feature of this plant is its prominent protruding stamens from the petals.

On the forest floor, pinedrops flourish. Pinedrops are a parasitic plant: they have no chlorophyll and their existence is owed to their association with fungi on the roots of conifers. Pinedrops can grow up to three feet tall and are adorned with bell-fashioned flowers blooming from the bottom of the stalk upward.

Within a half mile, the shaded north-facing slope houses fairy slipper orchids. These beauties bloom early- to mid-June and are scattered along the trail. Be respectful of the orchid family—observe, and leave them for others to enjoy.

Heartleaf arnicas along the trail.

Spotted coralroot orchids are numerous throughout this hike. You may find variations of colors of the coralroot from reds to pale yellow. Nooks in the rocks provide habitat for the common blue violet, white Canadian violets, and bracted alumroot. Macoun buttercups are footed in the moist ground. Blue-eyed Mary and the northern fairy candelabra often go unnoticed due to the delicacy of their tiny flowers; don't miss these small yet very attractive plants! On the other hand, the fragrant white waxflower and chokecherry shrub's

Low-growing pipsissewa features clusters of nodding pink flowers.

heavily-scented flowers are sizeable and showy.

Although it may be common, there is no question about the wild rose's surprising beauty. In the fall, the rose bush is just as lovely with fruits called "rose hips." Accumulations of wild roses are notable on this trail. Pipsissewa, one-sided wintergreen, green-flowered wintergreen, and twinflowers are low-growing plants found in shady, moist soil along the trail.

Cross a footbridge where white Canadian violets and wild sarsaparilla grow. Wild sarsaparilla has intriguing flowers hiding under the plant's large bronze leaves. The trail hugs rock outcroppings with steep hillsides below you dropping to the creek. Watch your footing here, as the rocks are often wet. Bracted alumroot again takes advantage of the cool rock fissures.

A unique flower, pinedrops.

The tumbling South St. Vrain Creek.

Pleasant walking with possible stream crossings (depending on rain) leads to clusters of whiskbroom parsley, golden banner, Richardson geraniums, Fremont geraniums, twisted-stalk, cow parsnip, miner's candles, and sickletop lousewort. Come to a fishing regulation sign where a small meadow accommodates larkspur and columbines.

A good stopping point is where Forest Service Road 252 intersects with the creek. Head down to the creek and relish the cool shade. Retrace your steps to return.

> **Bonus hike**
> Continue up past the creek junction for approximately 150 vertical feet to the junction for Millers Rock. The extra steps are worth it for the view and additional flower sightings, such as the britton skullcap.

5. Chautauqua Trail / Bluebell Mesa Spur Loop

CITY OF BOULDER OPEN SPACE AND MOUNTAIN PARKS

MAPS	Trails Illustrated, Boulder/Golden, Number 100; USGS, Eldorado Springs, 7.5 minute; Open Space & Mountain Parks Trail Guide, Mountain Parks Region, City of Boulder
ELEVATION GAIN	440 feet
RATING	Easy
ROUND-TRIP DISTANCE	1.6 miles
ROUND-TRIP TIME	2 hours
NEAREST LANDMARK	Chautauqua Ranger Cottage
PEAK BLOOM	June
LIFE ZONE	Foothills

COMMENT: Enjoy these easily accessible trails in historic Chautauqua Park. Views of the Flatirons, meadows, and ponderosa pine forest, along with the native wildflowers, make for a rewarding outing. The Ranger Cottage provides restrooms, maps, and a checklist of plants. Dogs must be leashed at trailheads and follow Open Space and Mountain Parks voice and sight rules.

GETTING THERE: From US 36 in the City of Boulder exit Baseline Road and drive 1.2 miles west to Chautauqua Park. The parking lot is located on the left.

THE ROUTE: The Chautauqua Trail begins a few steps from the Ranger Cottage. In the meadows, blue flax, yarrow,

The Flatirons tower behind meadows where the fluttering mariposa lily grows.

and mariposa lily are the first flowers to be seen. *Mariposa* means butterfly in Spanish; its light, papery petals blowing in the wind reminded early Spanish travelers of fluttering butterflies. No matter what the name, it is a graceful addition to these meadows. The yellow salsify shows itself, but wait, there is purple salsify, too! Salsify is a non-native plant introduced into North America from the Mediterranean. It may have had a purposeful introduction, as its roots are edible. "Goatsbeard" is another common name for the salsify.

Numerous shades of pink take over as wild roses (Woods') come into view. Named for Joseph Woods, an English botanist, this lovely rose grows from the foothills to the subalpine.

Pass the Ski Jump Trail and continue up to stands of lupine that dot the meadows. The Flatirons provide a striking backdrop highlighting the lupines' deep colors. Passing the junction for Blue Mesa Trail, the trail begins to rise gently to where the bright, orange-yellow faces of foothill arnicas are clustered. Sulphurflower, mouse-ear chickweed, golden banner, leafy cinquefoil, and many-flowered puccoon are scattered throughout the meadows. The many-flowered puccoon can be differentiated from the narrowleaf puccoon by its petals. Both have tubular shaped flowers, but the narrowleaf puccoon has fringed-edged petals and a narrow throat opening. The many-flowered puccoon petals are entire (smooth) and the flower has a larger throat opening.

Scorpion weed, northern bedstraw, britton skullcap, chiming bells, monkshood, and wild iris all bloom along the next portion of the trail. A flourishing garden of spreading dog-

The stunning beauty of the mariposa lily. Note the numerous color variations in the hairy center.

Beautiful lupine stands along the Chautauqua Trail.

bane, whiplash daisy, cutleaf daisy, and Lambert's locoweed fills the trailsides.

Houndstongue, a noxious weed, takes the opportunity to sprout among native holly-grape. Watch for poison hemlock, another noxious weed. Its stems have purple blotches that help distinguish it from other parsley family members that look similar.

A switchback leads to a signed junction. Veer left to the lower Bluebell Mesa/Bluebell Baird Trail. A pocket of mountain and Parry's harebells, pussytoes, and stonecrop dominates this section. Pass the Bluebell Mesa Trail and continue straight on the Bluebell Baird Trail to a series of steps. Wood sorrel is often seen here. This plant has funnel-shaped yellow flowers with folded leaflets. Tufted evening primrose and prickly pear cactus lead down to restrooms surrounded by ninebark shrubs. Swing left, passing the restrooms and

The uncommon purple salsify has elaborate stamens.

picnic tables, hiking the service road a short distance, and bearing left to the Bluebell Mesa Spur Trail.

Generous views are accompanied by beautiful meadows loaded with one-sided penstemon, wallflowers, boulder raspberry shrubs, wild roses, yellow sweet clover, and blanketflowers. Western spiderwort plants are abundant here, growing in clumps. Continue down past the next junction to meet the Chautauqua Trail, completing the loop.

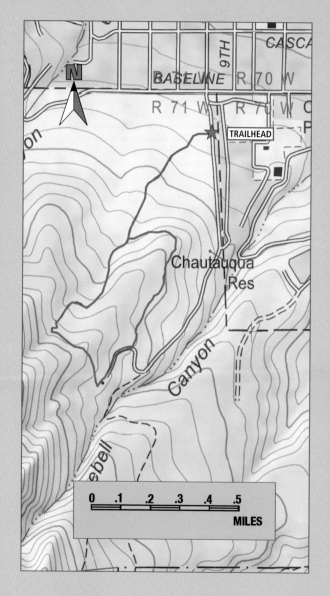

6. Coyote Ridge

CITY OF FORT COLLINS OPEN SPACE

MAPS	USGS, Loveland, Masonville, 7.5 minute; City of Fort Collins Coyote Ridge Natural Area Map; Larimer County Natural Resources Recreation Map
ELEVATION GAIN	600 feet
RATING	Easy
ROUND-TRIP DISTANCE	4.2 miles
ROUND-TRIP TIME	3–4 hours
NEAREST LANDMARK	Loveland
PEAK BLOOM	May–June
LIFE ZONE	Plains/foothills

COMMENT: This is an out and back hike where the prairies meet the mountains. Ever-changing hues of open skies, grasslands, and flowering plants against a backdrop of rising hogbacks create a fascinating landscape. In addition to surprising flowers, spectacular views from the top of a hogback await you. Interpretative signs along the trail provide valuable information about this ecosystem, adding to the day's enjoyment.

Pick up a free map at the trailhead. Restrooms are located 1.0 mile from the trailhead. There is also a cabin near the restrooms that is open only for educational purposes. An early start is recommended due to the exposure of the sun on this trail and the limited parking. Beware of rattlesnakes. Dogs are not allowed on the trail.

GETTING THERE: From the intersection of US 34 and Wilson Street (County Road 19) in Loveland, turn north on Wilson

Endemic bells twinpod. This plant is known to grow only in the Front Range of Colorado.

Street and drive 5.1 miles. The Coyote Ridge Trailhead and parking area will be on the left at Spring Ridge Mesa Road.

From Fort Collins, at the intersection of Harmony Road and Taft Hill Road, drive south for approximately 3 miles to the signed trailhead on the right at Spring Ridge Mesa Road.

THE ROUTE: This wildflower outing begins on a level dirt road. Immediately, prairie dogs appear, scattering through the grasses and performing entertaining antics. Note the sea of hearty grasses and their role in this environment. Soon familiar flowers appear: whiskbroom parsley, wallflowers, foothills milkvetch, Short's milkvetch, and prickly poppy. Sunlit faces of the common sunflower often pack the meadows along the road.

As the road winds south, prince's plumes appear with delicate yellow flowers fashioning plumes that wave in the grasslands. Look for this flower blooming in mid-June. Also blooming in June are early larkspur, white larkspur, copper mallow, Mexican hats, yellow sweet clover, yucca, winged buckwheat, salsify, and purple and white prairie clover. Snow

Plant life provides lunch for the prairie dog colony that lives at Coyote Ridge.

on the mountain, a native spurge, grows effortlessly in the dry soil.

At the top of a small rise in the road, the highlight of the outing waits. Coyote Ridge holds a rare plant: Bell's twinpod. This plant is endemic to the Front Range of Colorado. It is found in just a few places in Boulder, Larimer, and Jefferson Counties and nowhere else in the world! Bell's twinpod thrives in shale and limestone deposits. Look for the rosette silvery leaves and small four-petal yellow flowers. The best time to find it in bloom is mid-April through May. An informational sign on the trail provides facts about this rare plant.

Once you reach the restrooms and cabin, explore the area for fog fruit, purple-flowered ground cherry, salt and pepper parsley, mouse-ear chickweed, and blue mustard. At the cabin a short nature trail begins, 0.2 mile long, with interpretive signs about native plants and animals. Take in the distinctive smell of sagebrush.

Leaving the cabin, the trail becomes steeper as switchbacks enter scrublands. Appreciate the mountain mahogany, wild rose, and bitterbrush as these shrubs fill the trail. Numerous butterflies are often seen along this section. Redstem filaree, a noxious weed, mixes with chickweed.

Soon you will reach the top of the hogback. The Coyote Trail ends here. Wavyleaf dandelions, yellow nuttall's violets, and prickly pear cactus are a sampling of the plants sprinkled in the rocks. Take a rest to enjoy the views: east to the magnificent plains, and west to the Front Range. Retrace your steps back to the start.

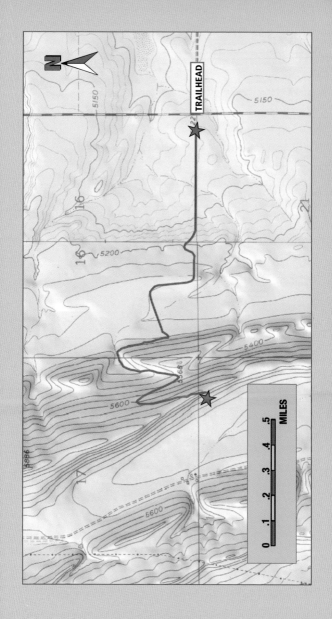

TRAILHEAD

5150

5150

5200

5400

5600

5600

5896

MILES

0 .1 .2 .3 .4 .5

7. Cub Lake / Pool Loop

ROCKY MOUNTAIN NATIONAL PARK

MAPS	Trails Illustrated, Rocky Mountain National Park, Number 200; USGS, Longs Peak, McHenry's Peak, 7.5 minute
ELEVATION GAIN	540 feet
RATING	Moderate
ROUND-TRIP DISTANCE	5.9 miles
ROUND-TRIP TIME	4–6 hours
NEAREST LANDMARK	Moraine Park Discovery Center
PEAK BLOOM	Mid-June–July
LIFE ZONE	Montane

COMMENT: Variety defines this loop hike within Rocky Mountain National Park. At mid-summer, more than 100 species of wildflowers are represented. In 2012 this area experienced a wildfire, which created greater plant diversity. Arrive early for parking as this area can be heavily congested. Dogs are not allowed on trails within the national park.

GETTING THERE: From Estes Park, follow US 36 west to Rocky Mountain National Park's south entrance. Be prepared to pay a fee. From there, drive 0.1 mile to Bear Lake Road, turning left. Travel 1.2 miles; turn right onto a paved road marked Moraine Park Campground. Directly across is the Moraine Park Discovery Center. Drive 0.4 mile, turning left at the sign for "Trailheads." Drive 1.2 miles to the Cub Lake Trailhead. If this area is full, continue 0.2 mile to the Fern Lake Shuttle Bus parking area. Restrooms are provided at this area. Hike back to the Cub Lake Trailhead to start.

Wild iris and golden banner bloom in a meadow along the Big Thompson River.

On the return, it is 0.7 mile on a dirt road from the Fern Lake/The Pool Trailhead to the shuttle bus parking area and 0.2 mile back to the Cub Lake Trailhead.

THE ROUTE: Begin by crossing a bridge on a level trail where shrubby cinquefoil, black-eyed Susans, and wallflowers are on display. Spring brings several species of violets, hollygrape, lanceleaf spring beauty, sagebrush buttercups, mouse-ear chickweed, and early blue daisy. In early summer, wild iris and golden banner fill the meadows.

Cross a second bridge over the Big Thompson River and immediately start looking for shooting stars. In July, two species of the Bellflower family are present: the common mountain harebell, with flowers that hang down, and the less common Parry's harebell, with deeper shades of purple and flowers facing upwards. Chiming bells, beardless one-

Meadow filled with golden banner, with the Continental Divide as backdrop.

sided penstemon, bluemist penstemon, Fremont geranium, Richardson geranium, and wild roses beautify the trail's start. Know your composites! This trail is plentiful with the *Asteraceae* (sunflower) family, considered to be the largest family of flowering plants.

A series of steps surrounded by rock outcroppings make a perfect home for the golden-yellow stonecrop. Owl clover blooms along this segment in July, adding interest. The sweet fragrance of chokecherry blossoms fills the air.

The trail swings west where whiplash daisies, star Solomon's seal, false (plume) Solomon's seal, and Wyoming paintbrush flourish. Ponds dot the trail where the white checkermallow grows. Goldenglow, frequently called cone-flower, quickly catches your attention. Britton skullcap, mountain blue-eyed grass, clematis, and the dainty blue-eyed Mary on a reddish stem pose along this section, with patches of meadow anemone.

At 1.7 miles, the trail becomes rocky, with uphill switch-backs along the murmuring Cub Creek. Here mariposa lily, heartleaf arnica, twisted-stalk, monkshood, cow parsnip, giant lousewort, tall chiming bells, horsemint, and other mint family species are found among the aspen groves. Fire-weed shows off its brilliance in late summer.

A campsite sign signals Cub Lake is near. Golden smoke and yellow pond lilies welcome you. Hike the north shore-line, ascending a ridge where dogbane abundantly grows, overlooking Cub Lake. Continue west to a sign marked "The Pool" 1 mile (right). As the trail descends, alumroot and spotted saxifrage cling to rock crevices.

Cross a substantial footbridge. Watch for delicate fairy bells hidden in the foliage. Western clematis vines weave among branches. Continuing down the trail, pipsissewa, spotted coralroots, white/green bog orchids, one-sided wintergreen, and bishop's cap mitrewort stand out in wet spaces. Before entering a small meadow, be alert for uncommon plants: rattlesnake plantain, heart-

Fairy Bells are found in the moist, shaded forest.

Wyoming paintbrush watches over Cub Lake, which is teeming with yellow pond lilies.

leaved twayblade orchids, and twinflowers. The trail winds northeast to The Pool. The Pool is a natural feature of deeply carved granite bowls swirling with turbulent water in the fast-moving Big Thompson River, an excellent setting for lunch.

Cross the bridge at The Pool and continue on a flower-filled trail following the Big Thompson River for 1.7 miles to the finish. Approximately 1.0 mile from the end, the trail winds through massive boulders fittingly named Arch Rocks. Meadow anemones, wild roses, prickly pear cactus, and Colorado columbines make an attractive finale.

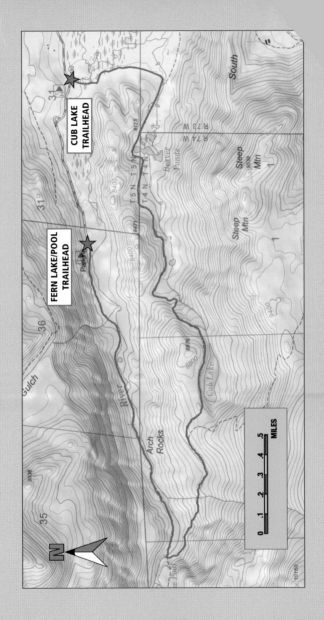

CUB LAKE
TRAILHEAD

FERN LAKE/POOL
TRAILHEAD

South

Steep
Mtn

Steep
Mtn

Beaver
Ponds

Cub Lake

Arch
Rocks

River

Gulch

N

MILES

0 .1 .2 .3 .4 .5

amond Lake

INDIAN PEAKS WILDERNESS

MAPS	Trails Illustrated, Indian Peaks/ Gold Hill, Number 102; USGS, East Portal, 7.5 minute
ELEVATION GAIN	1,222 feet
RATING	Moderate
ROUND-TRIP DISTANCE	4.6 miles
ROUND-TRIP TIME	4–5 hours
NEAREST LANDMARK	Town of Eldora
PEAK BLOOM	Mid-July–August
LIFE ZONE	Subalpine

COMMENT: Diamond Lake is a popular destination located in the Indian Peaks Wilderness. The best approach is from the Fourth of July Trailhead; this trail is heavily used, so plan an early start as parking is limited. This trail gains and loses elevation both coming and going. Diamond Lake is at 10,940 feet. In July you will see over 100 species of wildflowers, making this destination a "must do" for wildflower enthusiasts.

GETTING THERE: From the junction of Colorado 119 and CO 72 in the town of Nederland, drive south for 0.5 mile. Turn right onto County Road 130, following signs to the town of Eldora. Continue west through Eldora; the road will turn to dirt. Go right at the fork (left goes to Hessie Trailhead) and drive 4.8 miles. This dirt road is very rough and may require a four-wheel-drive vehicle. For road information call the Boulder Ranger District at 303-541-2500. The parking area is uphill past the restrooms. Dogs are allowed on leash.

Cascading waterfall with Parry's primroses.

THE ROUTE: On the drive up, watch for locoweed and white fairy trumpet. You may see hybrids of the white (white gilia) and red fairy trumpet (scarlet gilia) in pink form. The creamy-colored subalpine buckwheat, goldenglow, and black-eyed Susans are also common along this road.

Start the hike at the Arapaho Pass Trail (#975). As the trail gently climbs, chiming bells, rayless arnicas, Richardson geranium, bracted lousewort, sickletop lousewort, northern bedstraw, mountain harebells, purple fringe, false (plume) Solomon seal, heartleaf arnica, penstemons, mountain death camas, pearly everlasting, and yarrow welcome you. In late summer, add the highly visible fireweed. Farther up, Colorado columbines and scarlet paintbrushes beautify the meadows. Under coniferous trees find Jacob's ladder with fern-like leaves and shades of blue to pink petals.

Continue along switchbacks where stonecrop and Fendler's sandwort reside. The trail levels out with bright faces of

Bright faces of the aspen sunflowers along the trail.

aspen sunflowers guarding both sides, making passage for Whipple's penstemons in creamy whites and dark maroons.

You will find both whiskbroom and mountain parsley along the trailside. Pink pussytoes and goldenrod join in. The cow parsnip's sizeable white flower, mingled with the regal purple of monkshood, deep blue larkspurs, and bright yellow rays of the tall triangularleaf senecios, create a spectacular show.

Diamond Lake surrounded by a variety of flora.

Dazzling glacier lilies.

Where timbers line the trail, look for the petite wood nymph. As you pass seeps and streams on steep open slopes, be observant of the minute bishop's cap (mitrewort). Willowherb, fringed grass-of-Parnassus, white bog orchids, brook saxifrage, and twisted-stalk all fancy this habitat.

Soon there is a widespread cascade of water gushing across the trail. Watch your footing, as moss covers the rocks, making them tricky to negotiate. Monkeyflowers, Parry's primroses, and shooting stars are often found around this stream crossing.

After approximately 1.0 mile, the junction for Arapaho Pass comes into view. In mid-June, depending on snowmelt, a dazzling vision of glacier lilies covers the hillsides at this junction. Conspicuous shooting stars flag the slopes, adding to your delight. Farther along, white bog orchids mix with elephantella to satisfy the eye.

Head left (south) and down, leaving the Arapaho Pass Trail. The trail loses 240 feet of elevation leading to bogs and South Boulder Creek. Upstream, a cascading waterfall dances, sheltering water-loving flora. Take a moment to explore, finding marsh marigolds, globeflowers, and magenta shades of Parry's primroses.

Back on the main trail, cross the bridge and immediately come to a series of wooden planks. As you cross the first set of planks, look for the green-flowered heart-leaved twayblade orchid. Colorado botanist Joyce Gellhorn nicknamed these delicate orchids "Dancing Ladies." Using a hand lens, the

A colorful bouquet above the lake.

shape of the "dancing lady" becomes visible. Nearby, the one-sided wintergreen hides under foliage.

As the trail gains altitude, damp meadows filled with aquatic caltha-flowered buttercups and Parry's primroses supply color. A larger meadow follows, presenting a bouquet of rose crown, elephantella, alpine speedwell, and much more. Keep a sharp eye for the pygmy bitterroot along this section.

Over a rise Diamond Lake appears with impressive views. Some of the flora that adorn this subalpine lake are mountain laurel, scarlet/rosy/western paintbrushes, king's crown, lavender subalpine daisies, and tall valerian. Retrace your steps back to the trailhead.

Bonus hike

Follow the north shore to a cascade emptying into the lake and hike up a "social" trail, or user-created trail, to higher flower-filled meadows. Snowball saxifrage, star gentian, Parry's lousewort, and the barrel-shaped Parry's gentian can be found.

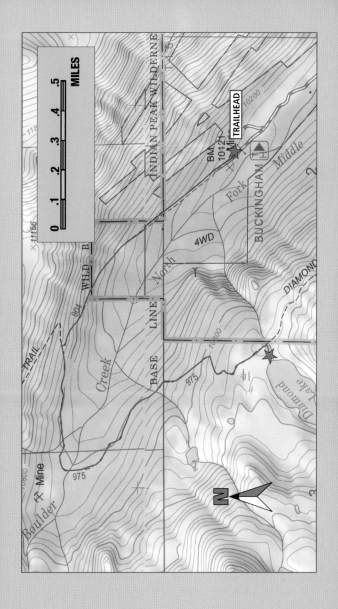

9. Elk Park Trail / North Fork of French Creek

PIKE NATIONAL FOREST

MAPS	Trails Illustrated, Pikes Peak/Canon City, Number 137; USGS, Pikes Peak, 7.5 minute
ELEVATION GAIN	1,200 feet on the return
RATING	Moderate
ROUND-TRIP DISTANCE	4 miles
ROUND-TRIP TIME	3–4 hours
NEAREST LANDMARK	Pikes Peak Tollbooth
PEAK BLOOM	Mid-June to mid-July
LIFE ZONE	Alpine/subalpine/montane

COMMENT: The slopes of Pikes Peak, known as "America's Mountain," have been luring hikers for over one hundred years with majestic features and superb spreads of wildflowers. The 14,110-foot peak is composed of Pikes Peak Batholith rock, resulting in coarse granite that supports several endemic plants. This well-maintained trail traverses alpine to montane life zones, offering a variety of flora along the way.

Be prepared for extreme weather even during summer months. Sturdy footwear is recommended for the uneven gravelly terrain. Note that the elevation gain is on the return. There are restrooms at the tollbooth entrance and at the Forest Service Visitor Center along the road. Dogs are allowed on leash.

GETTING THERE: From Interstate 25 in Colorado Springs, exit US 24 west (Cimarron Street) and drive 9 miles. Turn left on

The alpine dwarf columbine has distinctive hooked spurs.

Pikes Peak Hwy/North Pole and follow signs on Pikes Peak Highway to the tollgate. Be prepared to pay an entrance fee. Drive 13 miles, passing the Glen Cove Store. Enter a sharp switchback just past mile marker 13, watching for a dirt road to the left. This left-hand turn to the trailhead is easy to miss, because it appears you will be driving into thin air; watch for metal posts marking the turn. Park at the first parking area where the trailhead is located, or around the bend at a higher parking area.

THE ROUTE: A sea of weathered granite supports a vast plant community combined with spectacular views. At 12,000 feet, this unspoiled alpine start embraces creamy alpine thistles, alpine sandwort, alpine bistort, king's crown, alpine avens, alpine mountain sorrel, sky pilot, and the sweet scent of

Mats of mountain dryads.

rock-jasmine. Pikes Peak alpine bluebells, *mertensia alpina*, appear from your first steps on the trail. This alpine plant, with deep sky-blue miniature tubular flowers on a short stem, rivals the alpine forget-me-not. The luminous faces of the alpine sunflower will hold your attention while you are taking in the alpine sights.

Many small-scale plants thrive in this severe climate, including alp lily, fairy primrose, dwarf clover, moss campion, and pygmy bitterroot. Intense blue forget-me-nots dot the landscape among the sweeping slopes decorated with thick mats of mountain dryads. Generous batches of gold-flower enhance the floral hues against pink granite. Dwarf wallflowers, mountain death camas, alpine candytuft, and snowball saxifrage fashion elegant bouquets.

Pikes Peak alpine bluebells.

This alpine section is adorned with several endemic plants found only in the Rocky Mountains of Colorado. A member of the *Saxifragaceae* family, rock saxifrage grows only in limited locations along the Front Range from montane to alpine life zones. This beauty finds itself amid granite outcrops on Pikes Peak, creating amazing natural rock gardens with its violet-magenta flowers. Nearby, large rocks shelter dwarf alpine columbines. Look for deep lavender and white nodding flowers with hooked spurs; this is indeed a rare species of the columbine. Next, watch for the Pikes Peak alpine parsley found on these tundra slopes. Remember, these plants are rare, so please leave them undisturbed for others to enjoy.

Before entering the shade of aspen trees, catch sightings of mountain harebells, elephantellas, Parry's louseworts, Whipple's penstemons, and Hall's penstemons. Hall's penstemon is a delicate dwarf alpine penstemon quite at home in higher elevations. Its intense color varies from deep violets to dark pinks. This plant, too, is found only in the mountains of Colorado.

Farther down the trail, after the first switchback, find another endemic saxifrage, Hall's alumroot. This species of the *Saxifragaceae* family has many delicate cream-colored bell-shaped flowers fixed on straight stems rising from thick basal leaves.

Descend into the trees, where switchbacks lead to more Hall's alumroot snuggled into rock ledges. Waxflower shrubs begin to cover the hillsides as spotted saxifrage benefits from moist areas along the trail. Tall patches of fireweed make a

Telesonix jamesii (rock saxifrage) rock garden.

splash of color in mid to late summer.

Stay left at the signed junction marked Oil Creek Tunnel. Follow the trail down to find Jacob's ladder, lanceleaf chiming bells, stonecrop, mountain candytuft, Wyoming paintbrush, and one-sided wintergreen. Continue on Trail 652 down to the North Fork of French Creek. Marsh marigolds, globe flowers, and Parry's primroses welcome you at the creek's banks. The creek offers a refreshing spot for an energizing snack before starting back up to the parking area.

Hall's alumroot ivory bells.

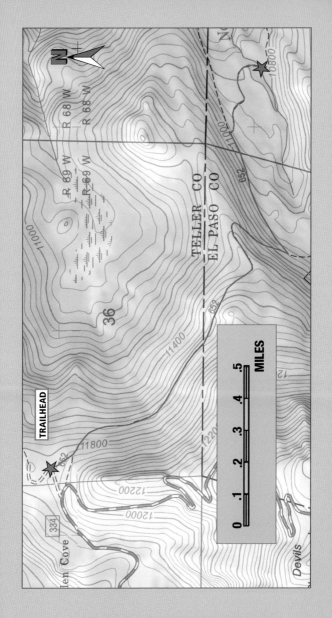

10. Horseshoe Trail to Frazer Meadow

GOLDEN GATE CANYON STATE PARK

MAPS	Trails Illustrated, Boulder/Golden, Number 100; USGS, Ralston Buttes, 7.5 minute; Colorado Parks and Wildlife Golden Gate Canyon State Park Map
ELEVATION GAIN	900 feet
RATING	Easy
ROUND-TRIP DISTANCE	3.6 miles
ROUND-TRIP TIME	3 hours
NEAREST LANDMARK	Golden Gate Canyon State Park Visitor Center
PEAK BLOOM	Mid-June–July
LIFE ZONE	Montane

COMMENT: The trails of Golden Gate Canyon State Park are a big draw for wildflower enthusiasts. A soothing stream follows most of this trail, which is chock full of flora. Shady glens of aspens and the trail's gradual uphill gains make this a pleasant hike. John Frazer homesteaded these meadows in 1869 after mining near Black Hawk. Be prepared to pay an entrance fee. You may encounter mosquitoes. Dogs are allowed on leash. The Visitor Center provides restrooms and trail maps.

GETTING THERE: From Colorado 93 turn west on Golden Gate Canyon Road and drive 13 miles, turning right on Crawford Gulch Road. The Visitor Center is to the immediate right. From the Visitor Center, drive another 0.5 mile to the Frazer Meadow/Horseshoe Trailhead on the left.

Mount Tremont overlooking early summer wild iris.

THE ROUTE: Immediately cross a teeny stream, finding Richardson geraniums, wild roses, and masses of shooting stars. Be sure to wander along the stream, finding mini-waterfalls surrounded by tall chiming bells and cow parsnip. Meadow anemone, lupine, red clover, and boulder raspberry shrubs adorn the uphill sides. Ledges form natural rock gardens for bracted alumroot and stonecrop.

At the first junction, continue straight on the Horseshoe Trail for 1.8 miles to the connection with the Mule Deer Trail. Fremont and Richardson geraniums bloom side by side. Britton skullcap, a member of the mint family, covers the trailside. Colorado columbines, with shades of deep blues and white accents, begin appearing; their unique and dramatic spurs make columbines a special flower. Many early-blooming fleabanes are found on this section of the trail. The heavily scented chokecherry shrub blossoms blanket the hillsides and later provide a bounty of dark berries. Goldenglow (coneflower) and blanket flowers add yellows and hints of reds.

Cross a small bridge where more columbines gather as the trail switches back into pine forest. The stream is now below you. Along here the full-bodied monument plant

One of many clusters of shooting stars along the Horseshoe Trail.

(green gentian) sprouts up, extending its tall stalk. This hearty plant only produces flowers once in its lifetime and then dies; its elegant flower deserves a closer look. Soon you will come to a spot where fireweed guards a footbridge. In addition, the spotted coralroot orchid is often found near this bridge crossing.

On the next switchback, drier slopes find the less showy pinnateleaf gilia along with sulphurflower, sawsepal penstemon, and Lambert's locoweed. This sunny site is just right for the spreading dogbane with its pretty pink clustered bell-shaped flowers.

Pink pussytoes guide the way up to the next junction. Stay left at this junction, where scarlet paintbrush, cow parsnip, white and pink geraniums, lupine, whiskbroom parsley, goldenglow, and beauty cinquefoil accumu-

Notice the intricate parts of the monument plant's star-shaped flower: four vertical fringed hair formations and dotted purple petals help attract pollinators.

late. Early in the season patches of wild iris abound. Cross yet another footbridge, where the often overlooked twisted-stalk's delicate flowers hang under slightly "crooked" or "twisted" stalks. After gentle switchbacks, a dead log in the middle of the trail points to the left toward a patch of red anemones blooming in June. Enter meadows overflowing with black-eyed Susans, aspen sunflowers, and many other flower families. Wallflowers with hues more orange than yellow collect throughout these meadows.

Flower-studded meadows.

The trail is beautified by black-eyed Susans.

Continue straight at the next junction following the horse-shoe signs. Leave the stream here to find a myriad of flora: paintbrushes, bracted lousewort, false forget-me-nots, healthy collections of columbines, and more shooting stars. Continue up these mesmerizing meadows until you reach the last junction before Frazer Meadow. The trail connects with the Mule Deer Trail within 0.2 mile of Frazer Meadow. Stay right on the Mule Deer Trail, soon crossing a footbridge into Frazer Meadow. Iris covers the scene in the early summer. Monkshood, along with a variety of other flowers, decorates the historic cabin, which is all that is left of John Frazer's life here. There are interpretive signs telling the story of John Frazer overlooking his flower-filled meadow. Retrace your steps back to the trailhead.

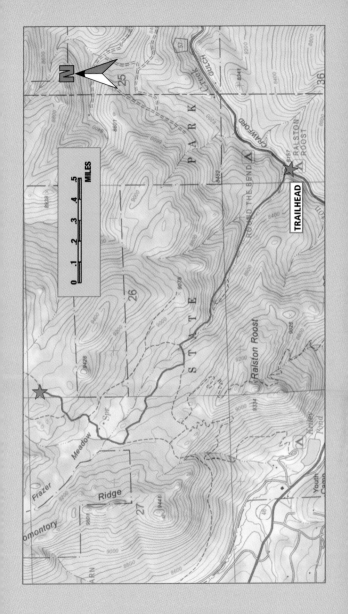

11. Lovell Gulch

PIKE NATIONAL FOREST

MAPS	Trails Illustrated, Pikes Peak/Canon City, Number 137; USGS, Mount Deception, 7.5 minute
ELEVATION GAIN	640 feet
RATING	Moderate
ROUND-TRIP DISTANCE	5.5 miles
ROUND-TRIP TIME	3–4 hours
NEAREST LANDMARK	Woodland Park
PEAK BLOOM	Mid–late June
LIFE ZONE	Montane

COMMENT: This is a pretty hike with a heaping helping of native plants. Pine forest, aspen groves, streams, and dry slopes make up the habitats that create the diversity of flora on this trail. The hike is described as a counterclockwise loop. The trail is well marked. In the right season, wild iris, shooting stars, locoweed, and blue-eyed grass dominate the landscape. There are no restrooms at the trailhead. Dogs must be leashed and/or have strict voice and sight control.

GETTING THERE: From Interstate 25 take the exit for US 24 and drive 17 miles to Woodland Park. In Woodland Park turn right on Baldwin Drive, which becomes Rampart Range Road. Drive 2 miles, passing several stop signs. The trailhead is marked with a small sign on the left. The Woodland Park Public Works and Utilities sign is a landmark at the turn for the trailhead.

THE ROUTE: Follow the "Trail" sign down, where stonecrop's brilliant gold petals and intense maroon stems pop out

Field milkvetch, Lambert's locoweed, and stonecrop are enticing to butterflies.

on the open, gravelly soils, enjoying full sunlight. Moving along, whiplash daisy, pussytoes, wallflowers, and Fendler's sandwort edge the trailside. The field milkvetch's lavender clusters mix with Lambert's locoweed and are a nice combination in the purple spectrum.

Incredible shades of locoweed are scattered throughout this trail. The white and purple species hybridize to produce a wide range of colors from pale lavenders to cloudy whites. Hike up the first switchback, where penstemons and beauty cinquefoil are seen. At the first trail junction keep right, where Fremont geraniums and Colorado columbines start appearing. The Colorado columbine became the state flower in 1899. It enjoys a wide range of life zones enabling the flower to be frequently seen.

Stay left at the Y in the trail, where yellow salsify, many-flowered puccoon, monument plants (green gentian), American vetch, and blue flax are plentiful.

Enter a refreshing, cool mixed forest with Wyoming paintbrush, golden banner, whiskbroom parsley, chiming bells, and western clematis. Mid-June finds nice-looking red anemones along this section. Wild roses and sharpleaf valerian

Colorado columbines, the state flower.

also make for a pretty mix. Stay left at the next split in the trail, crossing a stream. Along this streamside are just the beginnings of Richardson geraniums, shooting stars, and star Solomon's seal. Fireweed blooms in late July. Bear right at the sign marked "Lovell Gulch Trail Loop 3.75 miles."

The trail brings you to higher meadows filled with a variety of penstemons, yarrow, mouse-ear chickweed, and beauty cinquefoils. The stream meanders close by with congregations of starworts and more shooting stars. Take note of the pinnateleaf gilia, Parry's milkvetch, and lambstounge. Various heights of miner's candles are scattered about. Walk slowly so as not to miss the broomrape; this plant lacks chlorophyll and is parasitic on roots of other plants, mostly sagebrush.

Shrubby cinquefoils come into this view. Continue following trail signs to the left at the next junction. As forests and meadows intertwine, winged buckwheat, golden draba, and spotted saxifrage highlight the path. Large boulder configurations add character to this amiable setting.

A switchback to the left brings you to a gated service road. Stay left, following this broad path. Vistas now open up to Pikes Peak and beyond. The path follows fields of blue flax, Lambert's locoweed, rocky mountain locoweed, and bluemist penstemon as it drops away from overhead power lines. Watch for diamond markers marking the trail. Steep but short sections of the trail mixed with level sections continue with a range of flora.

Near the end of this loop, perky Sues and spotted coralroots conclude this flower-packed trail. Continue heading down to the junction to cross the stream, bearing right back to the parking area.

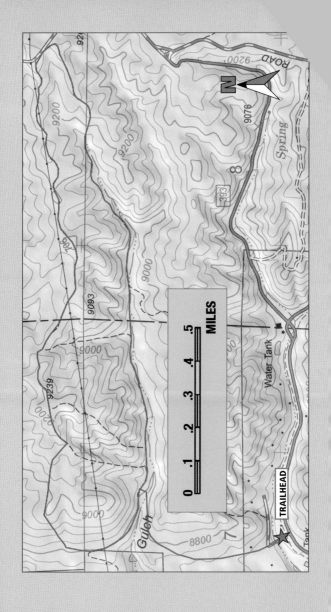

ldle St. Vrain/Buchanan
ail

ARAPAHO–ROOSEVELT NATIONAL FOREST

MAPS	Trails Illustrated, Indian Peaks/ Gold Hill, Number 102; USGS, Allenspark, 7.5 minute
ELEVATION GAIN	920 feet
RATING	Moderate
ROUND-TRIP DISTANCE	7 miles
ROUND-TRIP TIME	5–6 hours
NEAREST LANDMARK	Camp Dick Campground
PEAK BLOOM	Mid-July–August
LIFE ZONE	Montane

COMMENT: The Middle St. Vrain/Buchanan Pass Trail is located within the Arapaho–Roosevelt National Forest. This glacial valley housing the Middle St. Vrain Creek offers a wildflower outing suitable for all abilities. Bonuses include a waterfall and possible sightings of orchids. Dogs are allowed on leash. Restrooms are available at the campground.

GETTING THERE: From the town of Nederland drive approximately 17 miles north on Colorado 72, turning left (west) on County Road 92 at the Peaceful Valley/Camp Dick Campground sign. The trailhead is 1.2 miles from this point. Cross a bridge through the Peaceful Valley Campground, keeping left to a single lane road and crossing another bridge to the Camp Dick Campground. Continue through the campground to trailhead parking. The trailhead is 0.25 mile down the dirt road from the information kiosk.

Shooting stars are simply glamorous!

THE ROUTE: Even before you reach the trailhead, green and white bog orchids are found along a tiny stream near the information kiosk. In late summer fireweed flourishes, marking time until autumn's chill.

Hike west on the dirt road, coming to a sign on the right marking the Middle St. Vrain/Buchanan Pass Trail. Steer right, crossing a substantial bridge over the Middle St. Vrain Creek. The trail brings you to a flurry of columbines, wild roses, early blue daisy, Lambert's locoweed, clematis, holly-grape, northern bedstraw, larkspur, and a variety of cinquefoils. Mariposa lilies, blanketflowers, Fendler's senecios, Richardson geraniums, Fremont geraniums, Wyoming paintbrush, mouse-ear chickweed, and white hawkweed

Yellow monkey flowers.

generously fill the meadow. The monument plant (green gentian) grows tall, covered from top to bottom with its exceptional flowers.

In mid-August, you will find the rattlesnake plantain orchid where the trail becomes defined by conifer and aspen forest. These orchids have a distinctive white vein running down the middle of their basal leaves. The tiny, soft white flowers are usually aligned along one side of the stem. Horse trail signs mark the beginning of fairy slipper orchids, pink pyrola, pipsissewa, and one-sided wintergreen sightings. Yellow monkeyflowers and heartleaf bittercress provide a splash of

A sturdy bridge over Middle St. Vrain Creek.

color along this riparian corridor. The solitary wood nymph (star pyrola) and spotted coralroot orchids are numerous on mosses and pine needles.

There will be several culverts for crossing streams where triangularleaf senecios, cow parsnips, elephantella, chiming bells, white bog orchids, twisted-stalk, and brook saxifrage are spread across moist ground. Don't miss the tiny bishop's cap mitrewort growing along seeps.

Next, negotiate rocky and often wet crossings leading to a small meadow holding an assortment of pearly everlastings, scarlet paintbrushes, yarrows, Whipple's penstemons, and snowball saxifrage, all making a flamboyant show.

Eye-catching scarlet red paintbrushes.

The exotic and rare brownie lady slipper orchid.

In approximately 2.0 miles the trail comes to the first switchback. If you are lucky you may spot the brownie lady slipper orchid. If found, please only look—do not disturb—as it is a rare species. As the switchback turns west, take time to view the falls below in a roaring gorge of the Middle St. Vrain. Hiking above the creek, find yellow stonecrop enjoying the sunny slope. Blue diamond trail markers lead to more wet ground with rotten logs forming a perfect habitat for the heart-leaved twayblade orchids. In mid-summer, you may find broomrape blooming nearby. Makeshift log "bridges" are handy for negotiating the often muddy terrain. Communities of chiming bells, sickletop lousewort, and bracted lousewort increase in number along here.

The trail opens to a clearing, crossing a rocky slope where raspberry shrubs, blacktip senecios, scorpion weed, and creamy subalpine buckwheats prosper. Back in the mixed forest, monkshoods, speedwell, paintbrush, mouse-ear chickweed, golden banner, northern (rose) gentian, and Canadian violets create a wealth of color.

As you break out of the aspens, Sawtooth Mountain magnificently juts out along the skyline. In July these meadows spill over with Fendler's sandwort, shooting stars, golden banner, scarlet paintbrush, pearly everlasting, marsh marigolds, globeflowers, and many others. Continue a short distance to the four-wheel-drive Coney Flats Road, which makes a good turning-around point. Retrace your steps and watch for plants you may have missed on the way up.

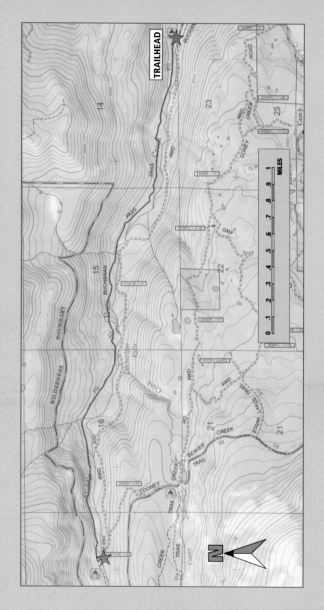

13. Mount Goliath Natural Area (Pesman Trail/Alpine Garden Loop)

MT. EVANS, ARAPAHO–ROOSEVELT
NATIONAL FOREST

MAPS	Trails Illustrated, Idaho Springs/ Loveland Pass, Number 104; USGS, Idaho Springs, Harris Park, 7.5 minute
ELEVATION GAIN	610 feet
RATING	Moderate
ROUND-TRIP DISTANCE	3 miles
ROUND-TRIP TIME	2–3 hours
NEAREST LANDMARK	Echo Lake
PEAK BLOOM	July
LIFE ZONE	Alpine

COMMENT: This is a stellar alpine flower hike to do in July. Traveling along the Mount Evans Scenic Byway, the highest paved road in North America, is an adventure in itself. The Mount Goliath Natural Area provides information on the resiliency of the plant life that prospers in this alpine setting. Life is a little more tender here on the tundra where extreme temperatures, severe storms, drought, and a short growing season are challenges for plant life. These plants have adapted with hairy leaves and stems to absorb and trap heat and long taproots to find water, and develop low to the ground to cope with strong winds.

Be sure to stop in and talk with an interpretive ranger at the Nature Center. The hike also includes a collection of ancient bristlecone pines, some more than a thousand years old. Hiking up to the Alpine Garden Loop requires sturdy footwear,

Enjoy the quiet of the alpine.

and you should have warm clothes in your pack. The hike is rated moderate due to the high elevation and rough terrain.

GETTING THERE: Drive Interstate 70 west and take Exit 240 in the town of Idaho Springs. Drive 14 miles on Colorado 103 to Echo Lake. Turn right on CO 5, the Mount Evans Road. A fee may be required. Drive 2.8 miles to the Mount Goliath Nature Center on the left. Restrooms are provided at the Nature Center.

THE ROUTE: Begin your hike at 11,540 feet at the Nature Center. Look around the interpretive gardens where information and flora examples are provided on alpine plant communities (fellfields, snowbeds, alpine marshes, etc.). You may be lucky to find the tiny moss gentian among the gardens. This tiny gentian will close with any bit of cloud cover. Head out on the trail where Fendler's sandwort, bluemist penstemon, alpine sorrel, pinnateleaf daisy, and stonecrop shape a great start. Walking through the ancient bristlecone pines adds a special gratification to the day. Find Whipple's penstemons in varying hues of creamy whites and maroons followed by shade-loving Jacob's ladder. Climb up the rocky switchbacks

Purple sky pilots enhance the alpine tundra.

where yarrow, mouse-ear chickweed, Geyer onion, dwarf goldenrod, scarlet paintbrush, rosy paintbrush, mountain harebells, and nodding ragwort make the most of the gravelly soil.

The trail levels off, with old snags providing a nice foreground to the picturesque valleys below. Clumps of mountain death camas, scarlet paintbrush, and many composites continue to brighten the path, while goldflowers, chiming bells, beauty cinquefoils, shrubby cinquefoils, and varying paintbrushes mix to create alpine mosaics.

Break out into open tundra, where rock crannies are packed with alumroot, alpine sandwort, alpine harebells, and alpine sunflowers. As the trail steepens, enjoy seeing purple fringe, alpine avens, and alpine buckwheats.

Stay right at the sign marking the 0.5-mile Alpine Garden Loop. Weave between large rock outcroppings with pockets of forget-me-nots, king's crown, pale yellow western paintbrushes, Parry's lousewort, sky pilot, big-rooted spring beauty, fairy primrose, and dwarf chiming bells forming

Clumps of pink moss campion.

perfect rock gardens, as only nature can create. The spectacular alpine big-rooted spring beauty, with rosettes of thick
reddish-green leaves and white flowers showing deep pink
veins, is a sight to behold. Add columbines to complete the
array of glorious alpine flora. Views of the 14,264-foot Mount
Evans and Chicago Lakes drainage come into sight, adding to
the stunning scenery.

Spring beauty is at home in the high, rocky terrain.

Bunches of alpine thistles are off-trail, meeting the road to the upper trailhead, which rises to 12,150 feet. Keep right at the fork in the trail, heading down to complete the Alpine Garden Loop and connecting to the Pesman Trail. Descending down, alpine phlox, moss campion, dwarf clover, alpine clover, goldflower, more purple fringe, and alpine avens await on the tundra as you retrace your steps back to the Nature Center.

Bonus hike
After your hike, continue up the Mount Evans Road to the summit parking area (14,130 feet). From there you can hike 0.25 mile to the summit at 14,264 feet, bagging a Colorado 14er while spotting more alpine flowers!

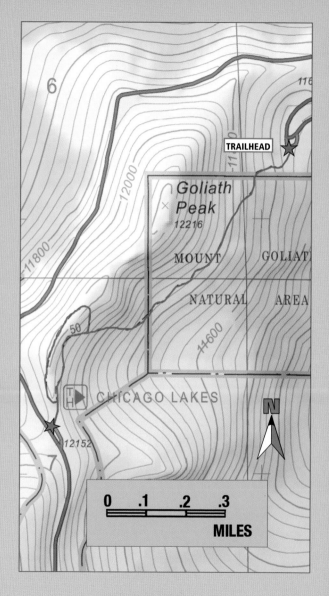

TRAILHEAD

Goliath Peak
× 12216

MOUNT GOLIAT

NATURAL AREA

CHICAGO LAKES

12152

N

0   .1   .2   .3
MILES

MT. GOLIATH NATURAL AREA
(PESMAN TRAIL/ALPINE GARDEN LOOP)   89

14. Owl Perch/Lodge Pole Loop

MEYER RANCH PARK, JEFFERSON COUNTY OPEN SPACE

MAPS	Trails Illustrated, Boulder/Golden, Number 100; USGS, Conifer, 7.5 minute; Jefferson County Open Space Meyer Ranch Park Map
ELEVATION GAIN	194 feet
RATING	Easy
ROUND-TRIP DISTANCE	2.4 miles
ROUND-TRIP TIME	2–3 hours
NEAREST LANDMARK	Conifer
PEAK BLOOM	June–July
LIFE ZONE	Foothills/montane

COMMENT: Meyer Ranch Park was previously a working ranch. Now this peaceful spot is part of Jefferson County Open Space. Easy access makes this hike a handy opportunity to explore the wildflower world. Don't be fooled—this short hike is filled with a wealth of native flora. The hike is suitable for all levels of walkers, making it a perfect excursion for the entire family. Benches and picnic tables are scattered along the trail, providing an opportunity for a snack and to study the plant life. Restrooms are located a short distance from the parking area. Dogs are allowed on leash. Trail maps are available at the parking area.

GETTING THERE: From US 285 south, take the exit to South Turkey Creek Road (right). Loop left beneath the overpass and immediately turn right following the signs. The parking lot is on the east side of US 285.

One-sided penstemons.

THE ROUTE: Meander on the road up to the trailhead. In spring, sugar bowls, golden banner, blue flax, and wild iris make a picturesque scene in these open meadows. In June, an interesting flower can be found among the grasses: pink plumes. Pink plumes is a flower wrapped with rosy pink sepals and bracts with whitish-green colored petals that droop from a slender stem. This flower is also called "Old Man's Whiskers" or "Prairie Smoke" due to its feathery plumes when gone to seed.

Chiming bells and elephantella are sprinkled along the roadside. As you continue up a slight incline, observe mountain harebells, sulphurflower, and a congregation of white bistort waving in the meadows. Bistorts have a distinctly pungent odor, resulting in their nickname "Miner's smelly socks." Stop and take a whiff. The unpleasant odor is a result of adaptation to high altitude. Bees are not as abundant in

Bunchberry, an uncommon plant found in Colorado.

higher altitudes as flies. Bistorts rely on flies as well as bees to
help in pollination, and what better way to attract flies than
with a "stinky" scent?

At the trailhead, follow signs for Owl's Perch Trail, turning
right to wind around the picnic area. Shooting stars, chickweed, white campion, Richardson geranium, and the more
common pink Fremont geranium surround this trail section.
Towering false forget-me-not can be seen amidst the aspen
groves. Geyer onions, with tight clusters of pink flowers giv-
ing off an oniony scent, alert you to their presence. Shrubs
of wild roses create a natural garden near the picnic area.
Salsify, pussytoes, whiplash daisies, whiskbroom parsley,
and Canadian violets wait ahead. Leafy cinquefoil, stonecrop,
wallflowers, and one-sided penstemon are colorful additions.

Stay right joining the Lodge Pole Loop Trail. Aspen sunflowers form an attractive boundary. Scattered throughout

this section are beautiful meadow arnicas. Soon aspen groves provide shade filled with golden banner, columbines, and Fendler's waterleaf. A covered bench forms a pleasant spot for sulphurflower, scarlet paintbrush, lupine, and more columbines. Cross a streambed where additional shooting stars, Canadian violets, and heartleaf arnica set roots. Do not miss the stout lance-leaf figwort (bunny-in-the-grass) on the right side of the trail.

Enter a mixed forest with multitudes of lupine, penstemons, Fendler's senecios, northern bedstraw, paintbrush, and columbine. As a switchback swings left, look among the pine duff for spotted coralroot orchids and pinedrops with bell-shaped flowers on a red stalk.

A ladybug is at home on false forget-me-not.

Bistorts attract flies as pollinators with their stinky scent.

Continue past the Sunny Aspen Trail junction, and head straight down for more sightings of pinedrops, bracted louse-wort, and rockcress.

A footbridge covering a large culvert is encircled with moist ground that is often filled with bunchberry. This flower is an unusual find in Colorado. Bunchberry, also known as dwarf dogwood, thrives in moist soils. Growing alongside is the dainty twisted-stalk and the moisture-loving lanceleaf-chiming bells.

Continue straight through this enchanting forest, coming to another log bench. Here a gathering of columbines, roses, and fireweed makes an attractive setting. Pass the next trail junction and continue left, descending switchbacks to complete the Lodge Pole Loop. Along the switchbacks, lupine, locoweed, winged buckwheat, and one-sided penstemon provide flamboyant closing moments. Rejoin the Owl's Perch Trail to return to your car.

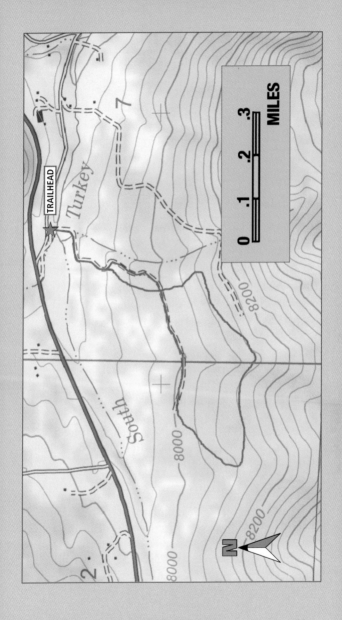

TRAILHEAD

Turkey

South

7

2

8200

8000

8200

8000

N

0   .1   .2   .3

MILES

15. Pawnee Buttes Trail

PAWNEE NATIONAL GRASSLANDS

MAPS	USGS, Pawnee Buttes, 7.5 minute
ELEVATION GAIN	383 feet
RATING	Easy
ROUND-TRIP DISTANCE	3 miles
ROUND-TRIP TIME	3–4 hours
NEAREST LANDMARK	Grover, Colorado
PEAK BLOOM	Late May–early June
LIFE ZONE	Plains

COMMENT: The Pawnee National Grasslands is located in northeast Colorado. The grasslands span 193,060 acres of high plains prairie. At first glance this area may appear uninviting, but upon closer examination, these high plains are full of dramatic flora and a landscape of varying colors. The quantity of blooms depends largely on the amount of moisture received in the spring. The grasslands are well worth the drive along this Scenic Byway route. You even may see pronghorn.

The Buttes rise approximately 300 feet from the plains and consist of carved bluffs and arroyos. Climbing on the Buttes is not recommended, as they are extremely loose and unstable.

There are possible closures of side trails from March 30 to June 1 for nesting birds. Bring a hat, sunscreen, and plenty of water. Have a full tank of gas before starting out. Be aware of rattlesnakes. There are restrooms and picnic shelters at the trailhead. Dogs are permitted on the Pawnee Buttes Trail but must be on leash.

Plains flax flower.

GETTING THERE: Take Interstate 25 north to the CO 14 exit. Go east 37 miles to Briggsdale. Turn left on County Road 77 (north), go 15 miles, and turn right on County Road 120 (east) for 6 miles to the town of Grover. At the stop sign, turn right on County Road 390 (Railroad Ave.), a dirt road. Drive 6 miles and take a left on County Road 112 (east). Drive 6.5 miles to a stop sign, turn right, and proceed another 2 miles, making a left turn onto Forest Service Road 685. Drive 1.8 miles to the trailhead parking.

THE ROUTE: On the drive from Briggsdale you may see fields covered with field bindweed. This is a common invasive noxious weed. Once at the trailhead, the journey begins on a flat trail with magnificent views of West and East Pawnee Buttes. Look carefully in the grasses for the soft yellow blossoms of the prickly pear cactus. White sand lilies also hide in these grasses. Bright yellow petals of the prairie ragwort are sprinkled throughout the mesas. The stemless evening primroses, blooming late in the day to avoid the heat, are frequently seen here on the dry plains. Wallflowers, yucca, and the prairie yellow violet begin to appear.

The trail meets a fence where the bright purple of Lambert's locoweed grows profusely. Proceed through the fence to find narrowleaf puccoon plants with frilly lemon-colored flowers. As you continue along, the matted white prairie phlox, also known as plains phlox, brightens the trail. The small bastard toadflax plant, with its white star-shaped flowers, is usually seen here sporadically, although it can grow in masses. As you wind up and down the arroyos look for the

Perky Sues give color to West Pawnee Butte.

less common white beard-tongue penstemon.

Don't miss the prairie loving plains flax. This flax is less eye-catching than the common blue flax and is often overlooked. The tiny flowers can range from a pale orange to a copper color with dark red centers. It is a delightful find. The yellow evening primrose brightens up the path along with the copper mallow, in orange sherbet tones, jazzing things up on the sandstone. On top of the washes, large mats of silky milkvetch form beautiful islands on the desert floor. The matted Hooker sandwort's star-shaped flowers also thrive here despite the harsh soil. Golden banner, whiskbroom parsley, and more wallflowers appear. The Louisiana bladderpod is found here, spreading close to the ground. Next find the spiked gilia, with tiny cream-colored flowers on a spike-like stem, which gives this plant its name. Perky Sue's cheery golden faces draw your attention out in this hot and dry environment.

When you come to the Lip Bluffs junction, continue left (east) to confront the West Butte. Here the windswept ground supports *oreocarya thyrsiflora*, common name "cat's eye," for its distinctive yellow center. This plant is in the *Boraginaceae* family, with the more familiar miner's candle. A few juniper trees add to the landscape. The easily recognized yucca plant is interspersed along here as well. Drummond's milkvetch and the uncommon prickly gilia expand here on the windswept soil. The matted prickly gilia's tiny blossoms only open close to evening. The turnaround point faces the end of the West Butte at the private land boundary. Retrace your steps back to the trailhead.

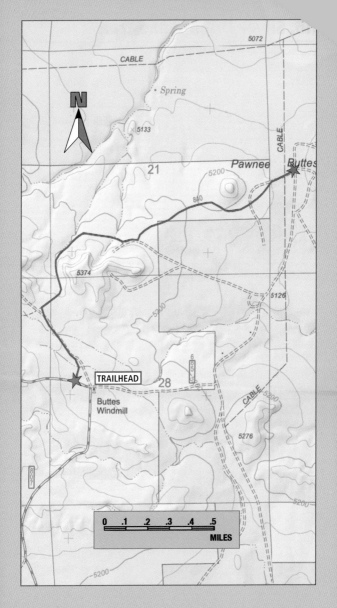

~~Si~~lver Dollar Lake Trail

GUANELLA PASS

MAPS	Trails Illustrated, Idaho Springs/ Loveland Pass, Number 104; USGS, Mount Evans, 7.5 minute
ELEVATION GAIN	1,100 feet
RATING	Moderate
ROUND-TRIP DISTANCE	2.4 miles (3.9 miles from the Guanella Pass Road)
ROUND-TRIP TIME	3 hours
NEAREST LANDMARK	Georgetown
PEAK BLOOM	Mid-July–August
LIFE ZONE	Subalpine/alpine

COMMENT: This trail is an exquisite jewel of the Front Range, encompassing a magical alpine setting, vigorously flourishing flora that cause one to pause and linger, and the fragrance of subalpine conifers and cool mountain breezes. June and early July may find the trail snow-covered in spots. Dogs are allowed on the trail. Restrooms are provided at the nearby campground.

GETTING THERE: Drive Interstate 70 west to Exit 228, Georgetown. Follow the signs through town for Guanella Pass. Drive 8.5 miles on the paved Guanella Pass Road. Pass the Guanella Campground and immediately on the right find the parking area. There is a rough four-wheel-drive road west of the parking that leads 0.75 mile to a second parking area and the trailhead at 11,200 feet. Parking is limited at both areas. Parking along the Guanella Pass Road adds an additional 1.5 miles round-trip.

Stunning Silver Dollar Lake is wrapped in wildflowers.

THE ROUTE: The long-blooming orange sneezeweed grows along the Guanella Pass Road near the parking area. They are recognizable by their large protruding disk flowers and bright ray flowers. If you choose to walk the four-wheel-drive road you will not be disappointed, as brook saxifrage, chiming bells, heartleaf arnicas, rayless arnicas, burnt-orange false dandelion, and nodding ragwort accompany you up to the trailhead. Many pass the nodding ragwort thinking that the flower is not quite open, but it is fully bloomed with numerous tiny disk flowers.

Ogle at handsome stands of monkshood, larkspur, and giant lousewort. On the roadside, it is common to find twin-berry shrubs, which draw hummingbirds to their distinctive yellow tube-shaped flowers, encircled by dark reddish-purple bracts. Their beautiful glossy black berries are possibly toxic.

Arrive at the trailhead parking on the right; across to the left is a trail sign marked Number 79. In mid-August watch

Nodding ragworts.

for the star and Parry's gentian, which grow close to the trailhead. Many species of paintbrush, yarrow, nodding ragwort, showy ragwort, monkshood, larkspur, subalpine daisies, and triangularleaf senecios envelop the forest. Elephantella is also seen early on the hike. Enjoy this shaded forest as a stream full of brook saxifrage among the willows comes into view. Parry's primroses, marsh marigolds, and globeflowers also fill the streamsides.

Switchbacks to the right leave the stream to find Jacob's ladder and fireweed. Enter a flower-filled drainage, home to larkspurs, monkshoods, triangularleaf senecios, showy ragworts, and Gray angelicas. A stream crossing sprinkled with bundles of Parry's primroses and water-loving heartleaf bittercress makes a nice contrast in the midst of conifers. Flat rocks help you negotiate the next stream crossing where one-sided wintergreen and bracted lousewort cover the ground.

The scene opens to a small colorful meadow that fills your senses with subalpine daisies, goldenrod, mountain harebells, mouse-ear chickweed, subalpine buckwheat, and scarlet paintbrush. Note the creamy blossoms of the subalpine buckwheat turning pink as they age. Tansy asters appear with deep lavender hues in late summer. Views expand with lupines and bistorts as the trail comes to a sign that simply states "Trail."

Stay on the main trail, being on guard for frail-looking starwort colonies. The trail continues up with blackhead

Parry's clover pours over sculpted granite.

daisies, alpine sage, snowball saxifrage, alpine avens, and yellow western paintbrush.

Magnificent grass and talus slopes aim toward the deep blue Colorado sky with an assortment of paintbrush, daisies, bistorts, and columbines. If you can pull away, mountainous terrain lies ahead with a bounty of alpine flowers. Peer below as privately-owned Naylor Lake glimmers in the sunlight. Alpine sandwort, spotted saxifrage, king's crown, kitten-tails, sky pilot, moss campion, big-rooted spring beauty, and

Parry's gentians thrive in the alpine.

The rare pink alpine lousewort.

Parry's clover blanket steep hillsides as marsh marigolds, globeflowers, and rose crown hold onto wet seeps below.

The procession of flowers continues toward the lake as you encounter steep but short, rocky, and often muddy sections of the trail. Alpine sunflowers, thick collections of triangularleaf senecios, and tall chiming bells cover the landscape. The infrequent pretty pink alpine lousewort is found among these rocky stretches.

Cross the outlet stream along the lake and see alpine goldenrod, Parry's gentians, northern (rose) gentian, moss gentians, arctic gentians, and mountain dryads. Find Silver Dollar Lake wrapped in wildflowers, making a grand setting for lunch. Retrace your steps back to the parking area.

Bonus hike

Hike 0.5 mile up to Murray Lake to find more alpine louseworts and in late summer, gentians.

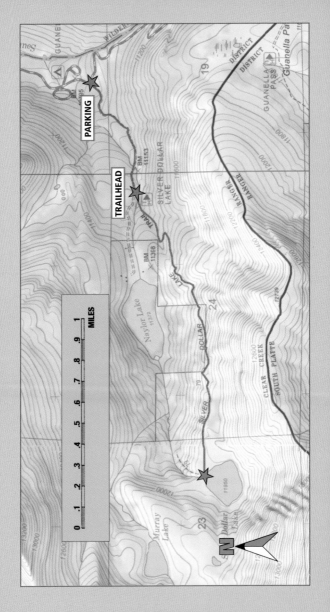

17. Sleepy Lion Trail Loop

BUTTON ROCK PRESERVE

MAPS	Trails Illustrated, Boulder/Golden, Number 100; USGS, Lyons, 7.5 minute
ELEVATION GAIN	670 feet
RATING	Moderate
ROUND-TRIP DISTANCE	4.5 miles
ROUND-TRIP TIME	4–5 hours
NEAREST LANDMARK	Lyons
PEAK BLOOM	Late May–June
LIFE ZONE	Foothills

COMMENT: Sleepy Lion Trail is named for a ranger who once observed a mountain lion sleeping on a rock along this trail. With the surroundings composed of dramatic cliffs and rock outcroppings, it's easy to imagine this sleeping lion. This trail offers a variety of foothill flora and enchanting scenery with views of the Ralph Price Reservoir and distant high peaks to the west. There are no restrooms at the trailhead. Please read the posted signs on park rules. Dog leash and control laws are strictly enforced.

GETTING THERE: From the intersection of US 36 and CO 7 in the town of Lyons, bear right (west) on US 36, drive 4 miles, and turn left on County Road 80. Continue on CR 80 for 3 miles to the Button Rock Preserve parking lot.

THE ROUTE: Hike west past the security gate on the dirt service road following North St. Vrain Creek for 1.0 mile to reach the signed trailhead. Prickly poppy, blue flax, bush sunflower, monument plant (green gentian), yucca, stemless

Larkspur in a quiet meadow.

evening primrose, salsify, and bluemist penstemon layer both sides of the road. The bright yellow flowers of the less common bird's-foot-trefoil (deervetch) grow low along the creek side. This is a non-native plant, a member of the pea family. Opposite the creek, chokecherry shrubs, boulder raspberry, wild roses, and Fremont geraniums

View of Ralph Price Reservoir from the Sleepy Lion Trail.

Showy faces of the foothills arnica.

line the path. Mid-summer finds showy milkweed blooms with lovely rose-colored flowers branched together on a large frame. Milkweeds are the sole source of food for the Monarch butterflies. Bracted alumroot hangs from rocky crags opposite the creek.

At 1.0 mile, on the left, you will see the sign for Sleepy Lion Trail, which heads south. A small seasonal stream runs below with lanceleaf spring beauties in May and shooting stars in June. Enjoy whiplash daisies, cutleaf daisies, pussytoes, mouse-ear chickweed, sulphurflowers, Parry's milkvetch, yarrow, and more Fremont geraniums as you climb a switchback. The switchback holds stemless evening primroses, mountain harebells, Parry's harebells, and prickly pear cactus. Spiderworts, Lambert's locoweed, mountain parsley, blanketflowers, and a variety of penstemons are interspersed among picturesque rock ledges.

As the trail enters a ravine, find wallflowers, lupine, Drummond's milkvetch, scarlet gaura, meadow death camas, and britton skullcap. Early season pasqueflowers bloom, announcing that spring is near. After hiking

St. Vrain Creek.

approximately 1.25 miles, thick stands of tall chiming bells make way for a large quiet meadow. Lambert's locoweed, foothills arnica, yucca, larkspur, and wavy leaf dandelions mix in the grasses.

The trail moves uphill back into forest past wild roses, nodding onions, common alumroots, and fringed sage. Negotiate through rock outcroppings as the trail switchbacks where spotted coralroot orchids are settled among the pine needles. Generous views of Ralph Price Reservoir and the mountains to the west appear. Early explorers named the two high mountains seen in the distance "Rabbit Ears," which today are known as Longs Peak (14,259 feet) and Mount Meeker (13,911 feet). A signed junction soon appears, connecting to Button Rock Trail. Bear right and continue on the Sleepy Lion Trail. Waxflower shrubs and dogbane grow profusely along the trail's rocky shoulders.

At 2.7 miles the trail heads north to meet the dam service road. Veer right on this service road situated in a small ravine,

Britton skullcap, named for the look of its profile.

a good spot to see pinnate-leaf gilia, stonecrop, one-sided penstemons, Geyer onions, scorpion weed, and Fendler's senecios. Find yourself next to a gentle stream crossing the dam outlet. Along here shooting stars and tall lance-leaf figwort can be found. This figwort is commonly known as bunny-in-the-grass, with yellow-green-ish-brown flowers that resemble the profile of bunny ears. You will also find numerous rocky mountain ninebark shrubs with their identifying peeling bark revealing many layers. White-pink-ish flower clusters cover the hillsides.

Reaching the North St. Vrain Creek and the main service road, head east for 2.0 miles back to the parking lot. Along this section of the hike, find one-sided penstemons, scarlet paintbrushes, blazingstars, miner's candles, and in late summer, fireweed.

Golden blooms of stonecrop beautify the trail.

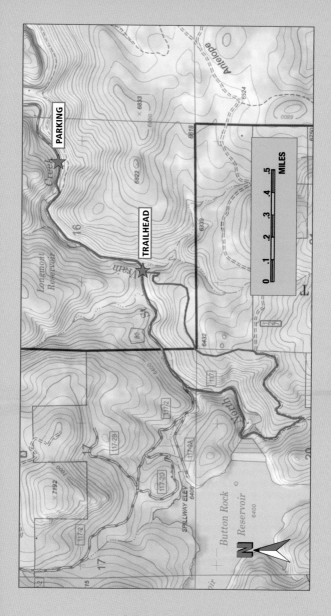

18. St. Mary's Falls

NORTH CHEYENNE CANYON PARK

MAPS	Trails Illustrated, Pikes Peak/Canon City, Number 137; USGS, Manitou Springs, 7.5 minute
ELEVATION GAIN	1,400 feet
RATING	Moderate
ROUND-TRIP DISTANCE	6.4 miles
ROUND-TRIP TIME	4–5 hours
NEAREST LANDMARK	Helen Hunt Falls
PEAK BLOOM	July
LIFE ZONE	Foothills/montane

COMMENT: The area surrounding North Cheyenne Canyon Park is stunning. The winding road to the parking area is lined with mysterious canyons, soft pink and red rock formations, and wildflowers. The trail consists of a riparian corridor holding thick lush vegetation, sparkling waterfalls, iridescent canyons, and tall pines, making one dizzy with inspiration. Add the history of Utes roaming this land and a collapsed railroad tunnel to complete a fulfilling day in the mountains.

Beware that the hike can be very hot in summer months, so bring plenty of water, a hat, and sunscreen.

GETTING THERE: From Interstate 25 in Colorado Springs take Exit 140 (S. Nevada Street). Turn right onto West Cheyenne Blvd. Drive 2.75 miles to the intersection of N. Cheyenne Canyon Road and S. Cheyenne Canyon Road. Turn right onto N. Cheyenne Canyon Road, driving past Helen Hunt Falls to the Gold Camp Road parking lot. Walk approximately 1.7 miles on the closed Gold Camp Road to the signed trail leading to the

A border of wild geraniums along the Gold Camp Road.

base of the falls. The nearest restrooms are located at the Helen Hunt Falls Visitor Center. Dogs are allowed on leash.

THE ROUTE: The hike begins on the closed Upper Gold Camp Road, an abandoned railroad grade. Gambel oaks, commonly called scrub oaks, are thick on the sunlit slopes. These tall shrubs turn rich yellows, reds, and oranges in the autumn months. Many-flowered puccoons, scorpion weed, yuccas, nodding onions, and salsify are found along the roadside. A member of the four o'clock family also is here, with clusters of light pink sepals/bracts, but no petals. Borders of pink geraniums get plenty of attention on the path. The hillside's

Scarlet gilia, a favorite in the foothills and montane life zones.

thin, rocky soil is perfect habitat for scarlet gilia and winged buckwheat.

As the road bends, wild roses surround North Cheyenne Creek, which flows down from above. Yarrow, northern bedstraw, pinnateleaf gilia, bush sunflower, mountain harebells, and the common dogbane enjoy this environment. Dogbane derives its name from the toxic sap it supposedly contains to keep wild dogs away; its leaves may be toxic to other animals as well. As you walk up the bend in the road, the vivid deep blues of sawsepal penstemon catch your eye. Notice the shades of pink deep inside the flower.

The road takes you up over a collapsed railroad tunnel where you wander up and over to a viewpoint. A metal sign appears for "St. Mary's Falls 1.6 miles Trail #624." Here the trail enters Buffalo Canyon.

Begin a gradual ascent in a beautiful valley beside

The striking sawsepal penstemon.

St. Mary's Falls.

a shimmering stream. Trout are often seen in the pristine waters. Wyoming paintbrush, black-eyed Susan, stonecrop, shooting stars, monkshoods, mountain death camas, wild roses, columbines, larkspur, and twisted-stalk find themselves near several mini-waterfalls along this passage. Explore the streamsides for ever-changing flora that seem to go on and on. The trail soon ascends to drier slopes where raspberry shrubs, common sunflowers, black-eyed Susans, and pinedrops are quite showy.

The trail becomes steeper as it approaches the base of the falls, which provide refreshing shade for a break. Continue for approximately 0.2 mile up switchbacks to the upper falls. Along the switchbacks yucca, blazingstar, and miner's candles bloom. Pretty and fragrant ocean spray shrubs (also called rock spirea) grow here, attracting butterflies and many animals that feed on the leaves.

Overlooking the valley to the east.

Impressive St. Mary's Falls stands before you, cascading down smooth granite rock, surrounded at the bottom by blue chiming bells benefiting from the mist. Timbers provide footing at the bottom of the falls to cross over the rocks and slabs. The views back down the valley make this hike worth every step.

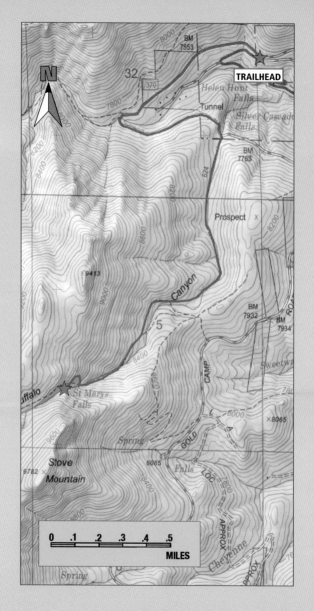

19. The Crags

PIKE NATIONAL FOREST

MAPS	Trails Illustrated, Pikes Peak/Canon City, Number 137; USGS, Pikes Peak, Divide, Woodland Park, 7.5 minute
ELEVATION GAIN	400 feet
RATING	Easy
ROUND-TRIP DISTANCE	3.5 miles
ROUND-TRIP TIME	3–4 hours
NEAREST LANDMARK	Mennonite Camp
PEAK BLOOM	Mid-July
LIFE ZONE	Montane/subalpine

COMMENT: A series of rugged granite boulders and cliffs of various configurations gives this hike its name. The riparian corridor of Four Mile Creek creates a moist habitat where flowers mingle with willows and shady aspens. Restrooms are provided at the trailhead. Dogs are allowed on leash.

GETTING THERE: From Interstate 25 in Colorado Springs take Exit 141 for US 24 and drive west approximately 15 miles to the town of Divide. At the second traffic light, turn left on CO 67 and drive 3 miles, turning left onto CR 62. Drive 1.5 miles, turning right at the Mennonite Camp on Forest Service Road 383. Drive 3 miles to the parking area on the right. The trail starts across the road.

THE ROUTE: This is an out and back hike starting at 10,000 feet, jam-packed with flora surprises. Cross the bridge where you will find shooting stars, columbines, and chiming bells. Take

Creamy-white globeflowers.

time to look around the creek banks for the shy wood nymphs hiding their faces among the foliage. Marsh marigolds and globeflowers also favor this habitat. Follow the trail beside the creek to find mountain parsley, Wyoming paintbrush, and Fendler's sandwort. Soon bunches of Fendler's senecios start to gather. As the trail becomes more steep, the easy-to-miss one-sided wintergreen hides in the shaded forest. Patches of stonecrop are scattered here and there. Now, above the creek, the trail levels where deep blues of the sawsepal penstemons stand out. Stroll along as the trail winds back to the creek, finding nodding onion and goldenrod. Thriving in between rock crevices is the endemic Hall's alumroot.

The dainty shy wood nymph, a common flower in shaded, wet areas.

Stay left at the signed junction for Devil's Playground and The Crags, 1.5 miles, marked Trail 664. Here clusters of white flowers on a bushy shrub announce the common red elderberry that later produces red/black berries. These berries are a favorite food source for bears. The wallflower, mouse-ear chickweed, and golden draba are soon visible.

Take a few steps off the trail to explore the creek's banks. Multitudes of marsh marigolds and globeflowers gather

Masses of pink plumes.

along the moist ground. More wood nymphs, fairy slipper orchids, plus star Solomon seal surround these banks. The small white flowers and slenderness of the starwort cover the damp ground. This little gem belongs to the pink family.

Back on the trail, several species of cinquefoil come into view, including the shrubby cinquefoil. Find the fragile

The unique rock formations of the Crags.

northern fairy candelabra, with its dense basal leaves, growing alongside the trail. It can be more distinguishable in the fall after its flowers fade and the plant turns shades of maroon. Bistort mixes in perfectly with yarrow, mountain harebells, and clustered penstemons. Looking for a hike to enjoy pink plumes? Look no further. Pink plumes, which are often referred to as prairie smoke due to their long feathery plumes when in fruit, explode along these meadows.

Tremendous rock formations flank the meadows as a variety of flora follows. Willows become thick and mingled with sharpleaf valerian, shooting stars, and more pink plumes. This species of valerian has conspicuous flower clusters on tall stems. The flower heads are often pink when first opening, turning white as they mature. Late summer brings several species of gentians.

Continue on the level trail with tall pussytoes, burnt-orange false dandelions, speedwells, elephantellas, and Whipple's penstemons interspersed in the grasses. Bear right, crossing a small footbridge where shooting stars, chiming bells, and cinquefoils are found.

At the foot of the crags proper is a good stopping point for this flower excursion. Here, at the first towering rock formations, find kings crown, a variety of ferns, and the rare rock saxifrage. The rock saxifrage, *Telesonix jamesii*, is known to exist only in three or four counties in Colorado. This exceptional plant puts on a magnificent show, covering rock cliffs with stunning, hanging masses. Remember, this is a rare species, so please only look and do not disturb. Retrace your steps back to the parking area.

Bonus hike
Check out the ancient bristlecone pines further up the trail on the summit domes. Enjoy the views, and along the way, columbines, snowball saxifrage, and giant louseworts can be seen.

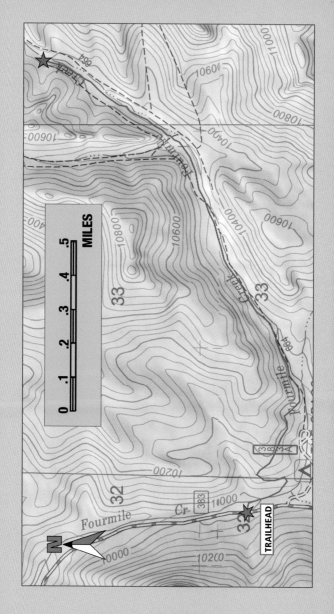

20. Tonahutu Creek Trail

ROCKY MOUNTAIN NATIONAL PARK

MAPS	Trails Illustrated, Rocky Mountain National Park, Number 200; USGS, Grand Lake, 7.5 minute
ELEVATION GAIN	640 feet
RATING	Moderate
ONE-WAY TRIP DISTANCE	5.8 miles
ONE-WAY TRIP TIME	4–5 hours
NEAREST LANDMARK	Kawuneeche Visitor Center
PEAK BLOOM	July
LIFE ZONE	Montane

COMMENT: In the 1800s the Arapahos traversed these mountains and numerous Arapaho names mark the natural features in Rocky Mountain National Park today. *Tonahutu* is an Arapaho word meaning "Big Meadow." The Arapaho word *Kawuneeche* means "coyote." The west side of the park receives more precipitation than the east, resulting in thick foliage and wet, large meadows. Mosquitoes are also more abundant, so come prepared. The route described here is one-way; leave a car at the Kawuneeche Visitor Center and start at Green Mountain Trailhead.

GETTING THERE: From the Beaver Meadows entrance station to Rocky Mountain National Park, drive on US 36 for approximately 4 miles to the junction of US 34 and Deer Ridge. Trail Ridge Road begins here. Continue on Trail Ridge Road for 38 miles to the Green Mountain Trailhead. At 20 miles you will pass the Alpine Visitor Center (AVC). If doing a one-way hike, pass the Green Mountain Trailhead and continue on for another 3 miles to the Kawuneeche Visitor Center. Park

Tranquil Tonahutu Creek traveling through Big Meadows.

a car there and drive another car back to Green Mountain Trailhead to start.

If you are driving from Grand Lake, drive north on US 34 about 1.0 mile to the Kawuneeche Visitor Center just before the Rocky Mountain National Park entrance. If doing a one-way hike, park a car here. Drive 3 miles north to the Green Mountain Trailhead to start. Be prepared to pay an entrance fee.

Dogs are not allowed on park trails. There are restrooms at the AVC, Green Mountain Trailhead, and the Kawuneeche Visitor Center.

THE ROUTE: The trail begins steeply, but soon levels to a moderate grade with 1.9 miles to the junction with Big Meadows and the Tonahutu Creek Trail. This trail has a spectacular start, with cow parsnip, monkshood, northern bedstraw, yarrow, aspen sunflowers, subalpine daisies, and Colorado columbines. A blend of chiming bells, lupine, Fremont geranium, mountain death camas, and pearly everlasting supplement the scene. At the first footbridge, triangularleaf senecios take over. Pass a second and third bridge where

Cow parsnip and monkshood border the trail.

shimmering heartleaf bittercress fills a small stream. At the fourth bridge, twisted-stalk grows with fragile bell-shaped flowers hanging under its stem.

As the trail levels, white hawkweed, smooth goldenrod, and dwarf blueberry (huckleberry) line the trail. Nearby is a pink carpet of the tiny twinflowers, a member of the honeysuckle family.

Sweet cicely, pink pyrola, one sided wintergreen, and heartleaf arnica flourish in lodgepole pine forest. The wet mead-

Elephantella dots the meadows along Tonahutu Creek.

ows alongside the trail are filled with elephantella and white bog orchids. Late summer brings displays of fireweed.

When you arrive at the Tonahutu Creek Trail junction, turn south (right) on the Tonahutu Creek Trail. Tonahutu Creek follows the trail for 3.2 miles to the junction with the Kawuneeche Visitor Center.

Watch for fairy slipper orchids in deeply shaded areas. Flamboyant meadows lie before you with pretty blue and lavender shades of the western Jacob's ladder, elephantella, clustered penstemons, bistorts, mountain harebells, and burnt-orange false dandelion. An occasional winged buckwheat makes an appearance. Big Meadows is surrounded by Whipple's penstemons, Fremont geraniums, yellow hawkweed, leafy cinquefoil, and Colorado columbines.

The Paintbrush Campsite sign comes into view with bracted lousewort, more twinflowers, and surprising clumps of wood nymphs. Note the slight willowherb and bishop's cap mitrewort along the trailsides. A side trip down to the creek is worth it, to find foothill arnicas, white bog orchids, monkshoods, bistorts, subalpine daisies, marsh marigolds, and globeflowers.

Approximately 2.0 miles from the Tonahutu junction, a small ravine with a seasonal stream supports western red columbine. This sophisticated flower likes to hide in the surrounding foliage; unless in bloom, it is easily missed.

The unique western red columbine.

The creek becomes noisy as it narrows and the trail descends to wild roses, northern (rose) gentian, and scarlet paintbrush. Brook saxifrage enjoys this moist habitat. After the Harbison Ditch crossing watch for reddish pinedrops rising from the forest floor.

Soon, you reach the signed junction for the Kawuneeche Visitor Center. Take the right fork and hike west 0.5 mile to the Kawuneeche Visitor Center. The last leg of this journey ends with more twinflowers, northern (rose) gentian, lupine, beauty cinquefoil, strawberry blight, and one-sided penstemon. If not doing a one-way hike, retrace your steps back to your car.

Mats of never-ending twinflowers.

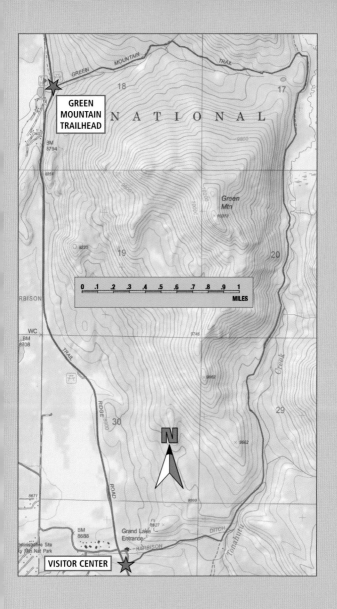

21. West Ute Trail

ROCKY MOUNTAIN NATIONAL PARK

MAPS	Trails Illustrated, Rocky Mountain National Park, Number 200; USGS, Fall River Pass, 7.5 minute
ELEVATION GAIN	1,038 feet elevation loss one-way
RATING	Moderate
ONE-WAY TRIP DISTANCE	4.5 miles
ONE-WAY TRIP TIME	3–4 hours
NEAREST LANDMARK	Alpine Visitor Center
PEAK BLOOM	Mid-July–August
LIFE ZONE	Alpine/subalpine

COMMENT: The hike begins at the Alpine Visitor Center (AVC) on Trail Ridge Road in Rocky Mountain National Park at an elevation of 11,796 feet. This is an extraordinary alpine wildflower hike starting above treeline and ending in the subalpine forest at the Continental Divide. In addition to a diversity of wildflowers, you may see marmots, pikas, snowshoe hares, and elk. Please be mindful of the restoration signs in designated areas.

A pleasant way to do this excursion is with a car shuttle, making this a one-way trip. This avoids uphill elevation gains and retracing your steps. Leave a car at the Milner Pass Trailhead (10,758 feet). Another car brings you back up to the AVC to begin the hike. There are restrooms at the AVC. Dogs are not allowed on the trails.

GETTING THERE: From Estes Park go west on US 36 following signs for Rocky Mountain National Park. Be prepared to pay an entrance fee. It is approximately 23 miles from the entrance station to the AVC following US 34, Trail Ridge

Alpine sunflowers are fondly known as "Old Man of the Mountain" due to the abundance of white, wooly hairs covering their stems and leaves.

Road. Milner Pass is 4.3 miles west from the AVC on Trail Ridge Road.

From the Grand Lake park entrance, go north on US 36 for 20.2 miles to the AVC. Be prepared to pay an entrance fee.

THE ROUTE: Begin by crossing Trail Ridge Road at the AVC parking lot to the obvious trail southwest. Follow this trail across the expansive tundra, enjoying alpine clover, dwarf clover, Parry's clover, blackhead daisy, alpine sunflower, alpine bistort, alpine dryads, spotted saxifrage, Fendler's

Snowlover, an uncommon alpine plant.

sandwort, and loads more. In mid-July, the petite elegant snowlover can be abundant and a treasure to find. Cushion plants, the champions of the tundra, are at home here, boasting their fortitude against the elements. Moss campion, alpine forget-me-nots, and alpine phlox are among these sturdy plants.

Within a mile, a rocky depression on the left (east) side of the trail shelters pikas and marmots. The pika's favorite food, alpine avens, are plentiful on the tundra. Just beyond, the goldbloom saxifrage, petals dotted orange-red, forms a bright carpet. See if you can locate an often overlooked plant,

Alpine sunflowers along the trail.

Sibbaldia, whose common name is cloverleaf rose. This plant can be difficult to detect with its tiny yellow flowers and leaflets resembling a three-leaf clover.

Farther on, three tarns create peaceful spots for burnt-orange false dandelion, pinnateleaf daisy, dwarf goldenrod, stonecrop, alpine sage, subalpine daisy, dwarf chiming bells, Whipple's penstemons, starwort, mountain laurel, Parry's gentian, star gentian, and rose gentian. Many shades of paintbrush color the tundra. In late summer, arctic gentians add to the mix.

After hiking 2.3 miles from the AVC, willows and krummholz mark the trail as you come to Forest Canyon Pass. Strikingly pink elephantella fill the meadows here. In July the Holm's senecio (ragwort) blooms nearby in loose, rocky soil.

The trail levels and is often muddy. Gray angelica, brook saxifrage, alpine speedwell, pimpernel willowherb, marsh

The dainty goldbloom saxifrage growing in rocky alpine soil.

marigold, and globeflowers enjoy this damp habitat to the fullest. Another find here is the fringed grass-of-Parnassus. Waves of brilliant yellow come into view with the triangularleaf senecio. The one-sided wintergreen shelters nearby under foliage.

At the signed Mount Ida Trail junction, swing right for approximately 1.0 mile down to Milner Pass. Along the switchbacks, robust masses of heartleaf bittercress show off brilliant white petals. Jacob's ladder and the elusive wood nymph grace the forest floor.

Rock cliffs and sharp spires are soon overhead. At this juncture, columbines, bracted alumroot, strawberry blight, alpine sorrel, and rock ragwort can be seen among the crevices. Blacktip senecio and purple fringe are in the assortment of flowers along Poudre Lakes at Milner Pass.

22. Willow Creek/South Rim Trail Loop

ROXBOROUGH STATE PARK

MAPS	Trails Illustrated, Deckers/Rampart Range, Number 135; USGS, Kassler, 7.5 minute
ELEVATION GAIN	200 feet
RATING	Easy
ROUND-TRIP DISTANCE	3 miles
ROUND-TRIP TIME	2–3 hours
NEAREST LANDMARK	Roxborough State Park Visitor Center
PEAK BLOOM	June
LIFE ZONE	Foothills

COMMENT: It can't get much better than stunning red stone ridges and pinnacles emerging from the ground to reach the skyline. What a backdrop to a spectacular display of early summer wildflowers! Known as a transition zone between the plains and foothills, this trail offers the opportunity to view a wide range of flora. A sign next to the visitor center puts it simply: "A tranquil and treasured place." Be sure to stop at this friendly information point. Benches are scattered along the trail, providing respites for taking in the view and observing the flora that surrounds this unique park.

Be prepared to pay an entrance fee. The park is open to day use only, so check in advance for park hours as they vary: 303-973-3959. Restrooms are provided at the Visitor Center. Pets are not permitted in the park.

GETTING THERE: From southwest Denver follow C-470 exiting onto Colorado 121 (Wadsworth Blvd.). Turn left on Waterton

A fritillary butterfly takes advantage of a burnt-orange false dandelion.

Road (past the entrance to Lockheed Martin). Waterton Road curves to the left and comes to a traffic light. Turn right at the light and follow Roxborough Road to the park entrance. The Visitor Center is 2.0 miles down the road.

THE ROUTE: On the drive to the Visitor Center, prickly poppies and yucca pose along the sides of the road. "Fried eggs" is a common nickname for the prickly poppy because of its deep yellow "yolk" center. The trail begins across the parking area from the Visitor Center. Scrub oaks and willows comprise the vegetation found here. Yellow salsify, larkspur, prickly pear cactus, and one-sided penstemon are seen from the start. Stonecrop grows on the dry hillsides alongside sulphurflower.

Stay right at the first trail junction to the South Rim Trail. Soon meadows spread out ahead, occupied by an array of native flowers. At the next junction, stay left where an impeccably placed bench delivers a pleasing view of a lupine-filled meadow. Soft purple shades of blue mustard

Native yucca plant.

also fill these meadows. This plant is an introduced invasive Asian species. Some say it possesses an odd odor; judge for yourself.

A footbridge creates a showy gathering place for golden banner. A gradual incline guides you to yet another advantageously placed bench offering a place to linger. Tall pussytoes, mouse-ear chickweed, yarrow, and larkspur are abundant. Butterflies add another benefit to this hike. Butterflies seem to be particularly drawn to the pretty burnt-orange false dandelions. Around a bend, more one-sided penstemon and leafy cinquefoil plants increase in number. Alumroot, false

Roxborough provides a distinctive setting for hiking.

Solomon seal, valerian, and many composites grow in sun-filled spots. Patches of Lambert's locoweed compete for the warmth of the sun's rays.

At the next fork off to the right a nook harbors a welcoming bench overlooking the lovely meadows. Pockets of britton skullcap, prairie clover, and the early blooming holly-grape are near this spot.

Continue down and left at the fork where Drummond's milkvetch, spiderworts, scarlet gilia, bush sunflowers, scarlet gaura, and blue flax occupy both sides of the trail. Copper mallow, often called cowboy's delight, blooms here.

Switchbacks guide you down as meadows provide habitat for salsify, monument plants (green gentians), mariposa lilies, and yuccas. This native yucca shares a mutually benefi-

Larkspur along the trail.

cial relationship with the pronuba moth. One species cannot survive without the other.

The yucca's fragrant flowers only fully open at night, when the pronuba moth is active to pollinate the plants. At the same time, the moths lay eggs among the developing yucca seeds. When the eggs hatch the moths feed on a small number of the seeds. The rest of the seeds mature to bloom again. Mother Nature does have it all together!

Stay left and cross a footbridge at the bottom of the meadow. Scarlet paintbrush and meadow death camas add to the mixture of flowers. At the final trail junction turn right to complete the loop back to the parking area.

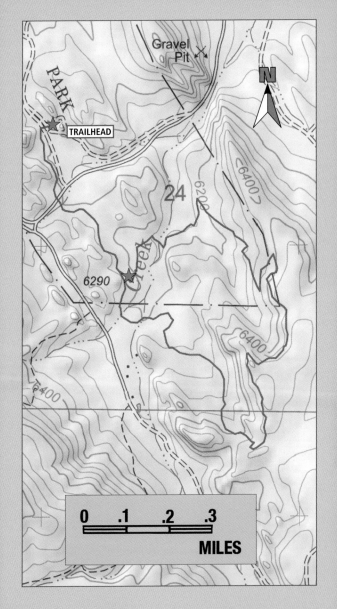

Gravel
Pit

PARK

TRAILHEAD

N

24

6200

6400

6400

Creek

6290

6400

0   .1   .2   .3

MILES

About the Author

PHOTO BY WALTER R. BORNEMAN

Marlene began photographing wildflowers and their habitats on her hiking and climbing adventures and gradually became interested in the botany behind the beautiful faces. Marlene has participated in formal class studies, informal groups, and extensive fieldwork to further her knowledge of Colorado's flora.

Marlene has climbed all 54 Colorado 14ers, the 128 USGS named peaks in Rocky Mountain National Park, and the 36 state high points. She has been a member of the Colorado Mountain Club since 1979 and is a member of the Colorado Native Plant Society. For the last three summers Marlene has taught a wildflower class for the Rocky Mountain Conservancy. Marlene has won several photo contests for wildflower and landscape photos. Her photographs have been published in the *Rocky Mountain Conservancy Quarterly*, *Trail Gazette* newspaper, *Estes Park News*, Aquilegia Newsletter of the Colorado Native Plant Society, and the Colorado Native Plant Society's yearly calendar.

Marlene holds a master's degree in Social Work and is a certified addiction counselor. She is the co-author of *Rocky Mountain Wildflowers* pack guide published by CMC Press. When not hiking Colorado's trails, Marlene and her husband enjoy traveling to explore the mountains and flora around the United States and other countries.

Appendix: Wildflower Common Names and Scientific Names

KEY:

Italic: Genus and species
Native
Noxious weed
Introduced non-native

COMMON NAME	SCIENTIFIC NAME
Alp lily	*Lloydia serotina*
Alpine avens	*Acomastylis rossii*
Alpine bluebells	*Mertensia alpina*
Alpine buckwheat	*Eriogonum flavum*
Alpine lousewort	*Pedicularis scopulorum*
Alpine parsley (Pikes Peak)	*Oreoxis humills*
Alpine phlox	*Phlox condensate*
Alpine primrose (fairy)	*Primula angustifolia*
Alpine sage	*Artemisia scopulorum*
Alpine sandwort	*Minuartia obtusiloba*
	Synonym: *Lidia obtusiloba*
Alpine sorrel	*Oxyria diayna*
Alpine speedwell	*Veronica wormskijoldii*
	Synonym: *Veronica nutans*
Alpine thistle	*Cirsium scopulorum*
Alpine willow	*Salix petrophila*
Alumroot (bracted)	*Heuchera bracteata*
Alumroot (common)	*Heuchera parvifollia*
Alumroot (Hall's)	*Heuchera hallii*
American vetch	*Vicia Americana*
Anemone (meadow)	*Anemonidium canadense*
Anemone (windflower)	*Anemone multifida*
Bastard toadflax	*Comandra umbellate*
Bedstraw (northern)	*Galium septentrionale*
Bell's twinpod	*Physaria bellii*
Bindweed (field)	*Convolvulus aryensis*
Bird's-foot-trefoil	*Lotus corniculatus*
Bishop's cap (mitrewort)	*Mitella pentandra*

Bistort (alpine)	*Bistorta vivipara*
Bistort (American)	*Bistorta bistortoides*
Bitterbrush	*Purshia tridentate*
Bittercress (heartleaf)	*Cardamine cordifolia*
Black-eyed Susan	*Rudbeckia hirta*
Blackhead daisy	*Erigeron melanocephalus*
Blacktip senecio (ragwort)	*Senecio atratus*
Bladderpod (Louisiana)	*Physaria ludoviciana*
Blanketflower	*Gaillardia aristata*
Blazingstar	*Mentzelia multiflora*
Blue-eyed grass	*Sisyrinchium montanum*
Blue-eyed Mary	*Collinsia parviflora*
Blue flax	*Adenolinum lewisii*
Blue mustard	*Chorispora tenella*
Bog orchid (green)	*Platanthera huronensis*
Bog orchid (white)	*Platanthera dilatata*
Boulder raspberry	*Oreobatus deliciosus*
Bracted lousewort	*Pedicularis bracteosa*
Britton skullcap	*Scutellaria brittonii*
Brook saxifrage	*Micranthes odontoloma*
Broomrape	*Orobanche fasciculate*
	Synonym: *Aphyllon fasciculatum*
Brownie lady slipper (clustered orchid)	*Cypripedium fasciculatum*
Bunchberry	*Cornus Canadensis*
Burnt-orange false dandelion	*Agoseris aurantiaca*
Bush sunflower	*Helianthus pumilus*
Buttercup (alpine/snow)	*Ranunculus adoneus*
Buttercup (caltha-flowered or plantain-leaf)	*Ranunculus alismifolius*
Buttercup (macoun)	*Ranunculus macounii*
Buttercup (sagebrush)	*Ranunculus glaberrimus*
Buttercup (subalpine)	*Ranunculus eschsholzii*
Calcareous cryptantha (cat's eye)	*Oreocarya thyrsiflora*

Calypso orchid (fairy slipper)	*Calypso bulbosa*
Checkermallow (white)	*Sidalcea candida*
Chickweed (mouse-ear)	*Cerastium strictum*
Chiming bells	*Mertensia lanceolata*
Chokecherry	*Padus virginiana*
Cinquefoil (beauty)	*Potentilla pulcherrima*
Cinquefoil (blueleaf)	*Potentilla diversifolia*
Cinquefoil (leafy)	*Drymocallis fissa*
Cinquefoil (shrubby)	*Pentaphylloides floribunda*
Clematis	*Clematis Columbiana*
Clover (alpine)	*Trifolium dasyphyllum*
Clover (dwarf)	*Trifolium nanum*
Clover (Parry's)	*Trifolium parryi*
Clover (red)	*Trifolium pretense*
Cloverleaf rose	*Sibbaldia procumbens*
Columbine (Colorado)	*Aquilegia coerulea*
Columbine (dwarf/alpine)	*Aquilegia saximontana*
Columbine (western red)	*Aquilegia elegantula*
Copper mallow	*Sphaeralcea coccinea*
Cow parsnip	*Heracleum maximum*
	Synonym: *Heracleum sphondylium*
Cutleaf daisy	*Erigeron compositus*
Death camas (meadow)	*Zigadenus paniculatum*
	Synonym: *Toxicoscordion venenosum*
Death camas (mountain)	*Zigadenus elegans*
	Synonym: *Anticlea elegans*
Dogbane	*Apocynum androsaemifolium*
Draba (golden)	*Draba aurea*
Dwarf blueberry	*Vaccinium myrtillus*
Early blue daisy	*Erigeron vetensis*
Elderberry (red)	*Sambucus microbotrys*
	Synonym: *Sambucus racemosa*
Elephantella	*Pedicularis groenlandica*
Fairy bells	*Prosartes trachycarpa*
Fairy trumpet (white)	*Ipomopsis aggregate*
Fendler's sandwort	*Eremogone fendleri*

Fendler's senecio	*Senecio fendleri*
Fendler's waterleaf	*Hydrophyllum fendleri*
Filaree	*Erodium cicutarium*
Fireweed	*Chamerion angustifolium*
Flax (blue)	*Adenolinum lewisii*
Flax (plains)	*Linum puberulum*
Fogfruit	*Phyla cuneifolia*
Foothills arnica	*Arnica fulgens*
Forget-me-not (alpine)	*Eritrichium aretioides*
Synonym:	*Eritrichium nanum*
Forget-me-not (false)	*Myosotis scorpioides*
Fringed sage	*Artemisia frigida*
Gambel oak	*Quercus gambelii*
Gentian (arctic)	*Gentianodes algida*
Gentian (green, monument)	*Frasera speciosa*
Gentian (fringed)	*Gentianopsis thermalis*
Gentian (little fringed)	*Gentianopsis barbellata*
Gentian (moss)	*Gentiana prostrate*
Gentian (northern or rose)	*Gentianella amarelle*
Synonym:	*Gentianella acuta*
Gentian (Parry's)	*Gentiana parryi*
Gentian (star)	*Swertia perennis*
Geranium (Fremont)	*Geranium caespitosum*
Geranium (Richardson)	*Geranium richardsonii*
Geyer onion	*Allium geyeri*
Giant lousewort	*Pedicularis procera*
Glacier lily (snow)	*Erthronium grandiflorum*
Globeflower	*Trollius albiflorus*
Gold sunspots (small)	*Tonestus pygmaeus*
Goldbloom saxifrage	*Saxifraga chrysantha*
Synonym:	*Hirculus serpyllifolius*
Golden banner	*Thermopsis montana*
	Thermopsis divaricarpa
Goldenglow (cutleaf coneflower)	*Rudbeckia laciniata*
var.:	*ampla*

Goldflower	*Tetraneuris acaulis* var.: *caespitosa*
Goldenrod (alpine)	*Solidago simplex*
Goldenrod (dwarf)	*Solidago nana*
Goldenrod (smooth)	*Solidago multiradiata*
Golden smoke	*Corydalis aurea*
Grass-of-Parnassus (fringed)	*Parnassia fimbriata*
Gray angelica	*Angelica grayi*
Green-flowered wintergreen	*Pyrola chlorantha*
Ground cherry	*Quincula lobata* *physalis*
Harebell (alpine)	*Campanula uniflora*
Harebell (mountain)	*Campanula* *rotundifolia*
Harebell (Parry's)	*Campanula parryi*
Hawkweed (white)	*Hieracium albiflora*
Hawkweed (yellow)	*Hieracium fendleri*
Heartleaf arnica	*Arnica cordifolia*
Hemlock (poison)	*Conium maculatum*
Holly-grape	*Mahonia repens*
Holm's ragwort	*Senecio amplectens*
	Synonym: *Ligularia holmii*
Hooker sandwort	*Eremogone hookeri*
Horsemint	*Monarda fistulosa*
Houndstongue	*Cynoglossum offcinale*
Iris (wild)	*Iris missouriensis*
Jacob's ladder (subalpine)	*Polemonium* *pulcherrimum*
Jacob's ladder (western/ leafy)	*Polemonium* *foliosissimum*
King's crown	*Rhodiola intgrifolia*
Kittentail (alpine)	*Besseya alpine*
Lambstongue	*Senecio integerriumus*
Lance-leaf figwort (bunny-in- the-grass)	*Scrophularia* *lanceolata*
Larkspur (early)	*Delphinium* *nuttallianum*

Larkspur (subalpine)	*Delphinium barbeyi*
Locoweed (Lambert's)	*Oxytropis lambertii*
	var.: *bigelovii*
Locoweed (Rocky Mountain)	*Oxytropis sericea*
Lupine (silvery)	*Lupinus argenteus*
Mariposa lily	*Calochortus gunnisonii*
Marsh marigold	*Caltha leptosepala*
Mexican hats	*Ratibida columnifera*
Milkvetch (Drummond's)	*Astragalus drummondii*
Milkvetch (field)	*Astragalus agrestis*
Milkvetch (foothills)	*Astragalus tridactylicus*
Milkvetch (Parry's)	*Astragalus parryi*
Milkvetch (Short's)	*Astragalus shortianus*
Milkvetch (silky)	*Astragalus sericoleucus*
	Synonym: *Orophaca sericea*
Miner's candle	*Oreocarya virgate*
Mitrewort (bishop's cap)	*Pectiantia pentandra*
	Synonym: *Mitella pentandra*
Mitrewort (side-flowered white)	*Mitella stauropetala*
Monkeyflower	*Mimulus guttatus*
Monkshood	*Aconitum columbianum*
Monkshood (white)	*Aconitum ochroleucum*
Monument plant (green gentian)	*Frasera speciosa*
Moss campion	*Silene acaulis*
Mountain candytuft	*Noccaea fendleri*
	Synonym: *Noccaea Montana*
Mountain dryad	*Dryas octopetala*
Mountain laurel	*Kalmia microphylla*
Mountain mahogany	*Cercocarpus intricatus*
Mountain sorrel (alpine)	*Oxyria digyna*
Mouse-ear chickweed	*Cerastium arvense*
	Synonym: *Cerastium strictum*
Ninebark	*Physocarpus monogynus*
Nodding onion	*Allium cernuum*

Nodding ragwort	*Senecio bigelovii*
	Synonym: *Ligularia bigelovii*
Northern bedstraw	*Galium boreale*
	Synonym: *Galium spetentrionale*
Northern coralroot	*Corallorhiza trifida*
Northern fairy candelabra	*Androsace septentrionalis*
Ocean spray (rock spirea)	*Holodiscus dumosus*
Owl clover	*Orthocarpus luteus*
Paintbrush (rosy)	*Castilleja rhexiifolia*
Paintbrush (scarlet)	*Castilleja miniata*
Paintbrush (western)	*Castilleja occidentalis*
Paintbrush (Wyoming)	*Castilleja linarlifolia*
Parry's lousewort	*Pedicularis parryi*
Parry's primrose	*Primula parryi*
Parsley (mountain)	*Cymopterus lemmonii*
	Synonym: *Pseudocymopterus montanus*
Parsley (salt & pepper)	*Lomatium concinnum*
Parsley (whiskbroom)	*Harbouria trachypleura*
Pasqueflower	*Pulsatilla patens*
	Synonym: *Pulsatilla ludoviciana*
Pearly everlasting	*Anaphalis margaritaceae*
Penstemon (bearded one-sided)	*Penstemon secundiflorus*
Penstemon (beardless one-sided)	*Penstemon virgatus*
	Synonym: *Penstemon unilateralis*
Penstemon (bluemist)	*Penstemon virens*
Penstemon (clustered)	*Penstemon procerus*
	var.: *procerus*
Penstemon (Hall's)	*Penstemon hallii*
Penstemon (sawsepal)	*Penstemon glaber*
Penstemon (Whipple's)	*Penstemon whippleanus*
Penstemon (white beard-tongue)	*Penstemon albidus*

Perky Sue	*Tetraneuris scaposa*
Pinedrops	*Pterospora andromedea*
Pink plumes	*Geum triflorum*
	Synonym: *Erythrocoma triflora*
Pink pyrola	*Pyrola asarifolia*
	Synonym: *Pyrola rotundifolia*
Pinnateleaf daisy	*Erigeron pinnatisectus*
Pinnateleaf gilia (sticky gilia)	*Aliciella pinnatifida*
Pipsissewa	*Chimaphila umbellate*
Pond lily (yellow)	*Nuphar polysepaia*
	Synonym: *Nuphar lutea*
Prairie clover	*Dalea purpurea*
Prairie phlox (plains)	*Phlox andicola*
Prairie ragwort	*Packera plattensis*
Prickly gilia	*Leptodactylon caespitosum*
Prickly pear cactus	*Opuntia polyacantha*
Prickly poppy	*Argemone polyanthemos*
Prince's plumes	*Stanleya pinnata*
Puccoon (many-flowered)	*Lithospermum multiflrum*
Puccoon (narrowleaf)	*Lithospermum incisum*
Purple fringe (silky phacelia)	*Phacelia sericea*
Pussytoes (pink)	*Antennaria rosea*
Pussytoes (tall)	*Antennaria pulcherrima*
Pygmy bitterroot	*Oreobroma pygmaea*
Pygmy tonestus	*Tonestus pygmaeus*
Raspberry shrub	*Rubus idaeus*
Rattlesnake plantain (orchid)	*Goodyera oblongifolia*
Rayless arnica	*Arnica parryi*
Rock saxifrage	*Telesonix jamesii*
Rockcress (Drummond's)	*Boechara stricta*
	Synonym: *Boechara drmmondii*

Rock-jasmine	*Androsace chamaejasme*
Rock ragwort	*Senecio fremontii*
Rose (wild)	*Rosa woodsii*
Rose crown	*Clementsia rhodantha*
Salsify (purple)	*Tragopogon porrifolius*
Salsify (yellow)	*Tragopogon dubius*
Sand lily	*Leucocrinum montanum*
Sarsaparilla (wild)	*Aralia nudicaulis*
Scarlet gaura	*Gaura coccinea*
Scarlet gilia	*Ipomopsis aggregate*
Scorpion weed	*Phacelia heterophylla*
	Synonym: *Phacelia denticulate*
Shooting stars	*Dodecatheon pulchellum*
Showy milkweed	*Asclepias speciosa*
Showy ragwort	*Senecio amplectens*
	Synonym: *Ligularia amplectens*
Sickletop	*Pedicularis procera*
Sky pilot	*Polemonium viscosum*
Sneezeweed (orange)	*Hymenoxys hoopesii*
Snowball saxifrage	*Micranthes rhomboidea*
Snowlover	*Chlonophila jamesii*
Snow on the mountain	*Euphorbia marginata*
Solomon's seal (false or plume)	*Malanthemum racemosum*
	Synonym: *Malanthemum amplexicaule*
Solomon's seal (star)	*Malanthemum stellatum*
	Synonym: *Smilacina stellata*
Speedwell (alpine)	*Veronica wormskjoldii*
	Synonym: *Veronica nutans*
Spiderwort	*Trandescantia occidentalis*

Spiked gilia	*Ipomopsis spicata*
Spotted coralroot orchid	*Corallorhiza maculate*
Spotted saxifrage	*Cilaria austromontana*
Spring beauty (alpine big-rooted)	*Claytonia megarhiza*
Spring beauty (lanceleaf)	*Claytonia lanceolata*
Starwort	*Stellaria longipes*
Stemless evening primrose	*Oenothera caespitosa*
Stonecrop	*Sedum lanceolatum*
Strawberry blight	*Chenopodium capitatum*
Subalpine buckwheat	*Eriogonum subalpinum*
Subalpine daisy	*Erigeron peregrinus*
Sugarbowls	*Clematis hirsutissima*
	Synonym: *Coriflora hirsutissima*
Sulphurflower	*Eriogonum umbellatum*
Sunflower (alpine)	*Rydbergia grandiflora*
Sunflower (aspen)	*Helianthella quinquenervis*
Sunflower (common)	*Helianthus annuus*
Sweet cicely	*Osmorhiza depauperata*
Sweet clover (yellow)	*Melilotus officinale*
Tansy aster	*Machaeranthera bigelovii*
Tiny trumpet	*Collomia linearis*
Triangularleaf senecio (ragwort)	*Senecio triangularis*
Twayblade orchid (heart-leaved)	*Listera cordata*
Twinberry shrub	*Lonicera involucrate*
Twinflower	*Linnaea borealis*
Twisted-stalk	*Streptopus amplexifolius*
	Synonym: *Streptopus fassettii*
Valerian (sharpleaf)	*Valeriana acutiloba*
	Synonym: *Valeriana capitata*
Valerian (tall)	*Valeriana edulis*
Violet (blue)	*Viola adunca*
Violet (Canadian)	*Viola Canadensis*

Violet (Nuttall)	*Viola vallicola*
	Synonym: *Viola nuttallii*
Wallflower	*Erysimum capitatum*
Wavyleaf dandelion	*Nothocalais cuspidate*
Waxflower shrub	*Jamesia Americana*
Whiplash daisy (trailing fleabane)	*Erigeron flagellaris*
White campion	*Silene latifolia*
	Synonym: *Melandrium dioicum*
Wild plum	*Prunus Americana*
Wild strawberry	*Fragaria virginiana*
Willowherb (pimpernel)	*Epilobium anagallidifolium*
Winged buckwheat	*Eriogonum alatum*
	Synonym: *Pterogonum alatum*
Wintergreen (green-flowered)	*Pyrola chlorantha*
Wintergreen (one-sided)	*Orthilla secunda*
	Synonym: *Pyrola secunda*
Wood lily	*Lilium philadelphicum*
Wood nymph	*Moneses uniflora*
Wood sorrel	*Oxalis stricta*
Yarrow	*Achillea lanulosa*
Yucca	*Yucca glauca*

A bouquet of wildflowers in Colorado's high country.

Checklist

THE BEST FRONT RANGE WILDFLOWER HIKES

Get Outside.

Become a CMC Member, today!

Explore the mountains and meet new people with the Colorado Mountain Club. Join us for trips, hikes, and activities throughout the state! Join today and save with special membership promotions for our readers: www.cmc.org/readerspecials

The Colorado Mountain Club is the state's leading organization dedicated to adventure, recreation, conservation, and education. Founded in 1912, the CMC acts as a gateway to the mountains for novices and experts alike, offering an array of year-round activities, events, and schools centered on outdoor recreation.

When you join the Colorado Mountain Club, you receive a variety of member benefits including:

- 20% member discount on CMC Press books
- 15% member discount on CMC hats, t-shirts, and hoodies
- 40% off admission to the American Mountaineering Museum
- Discounts at various outdoor retailers
- Subscription to *Trail & Timberline* magazine
- FREE signups to over 3,000 mountain adventures annually
- Access to courses, classes, and seminars throughout the state
- Adventure Travel opportunities to take you to the world's great destinations